What people are saying about

Pagan Portals – Scrying

A must have! A clear and concise [...] the art of scrying. Lucya Starza [...] steps necessary to be successful [...] great for beginners and is a g[...] more advanced practitioners.

Jennifer Teixeira, author of *Temple of the Bones; Rituals to the Goddess Hekate*

As someone for whom scrying didn't come easily at first, Lucya Starza's book *Pagan Portals – Scrying* would have been just the thing to help me get started. From clear instructions to helpful exercises, Lucya covers all of the questions a reader might have – and some that I hadn't thought about until I read the book. I especially enjoyed the considerable references that helped with content and added more ideas to my magical practice. Highly recommended for beginners as well as seasoned practitioners.

Irisanya Moon, reclaiming witch and author of *Pagan Portals – Reclaiming Witchcraft*; *Pagan Portals – Aphrodite: Goddess of Love and Beauty and Initiation*; and *Practically Pagan...An Alternative Guide to Health and Well-being*

Pagan Portals – Scrying is a practical guide for anyone who wishes to learn the art of scrying. From my own experience and many others who have practiced, everyone's approach to scrying varies according to which method a person may use. Moon phase, time of day, environment are factors among others that can affect results. Lucya Starza takes all of this into account, exploring the different modes of scrying and how to connect to the energies necessary for success. At the end of the book there is a useful section on problem solving and frequently asked questions for those who get a little stuck or disheartened. Worth the read.

Martha Gray, author of *Pagan Portals – Grimalkyn: The Witch's Cat*

Previous Books

Candle Magic
A witch's guide to spells and rituals
978-1-78535-043-6 (paperback)
978-1-78535-044-3 (e-book)

Poppets and Magical Dolls
Dolls for spellwork, witchcraft and seasonal celebrations
978-1-78535-721-3 (paperback)
978-1-78535-722-0 (e-book)

Guided Visualisations
Pathways into wisdom and witchcraft
978-1-78904-567-3 (paperback)
978-1-78904-568-0 (e-book)

Pagan Portals
Scrying

Divination using crystals, mirrors,
water and fire

Pagan Portals
Scrying

Divination using crystals, mirrors,
water and fire

Lucya Starza

**MOON
BOOKS**

Winchester, UK
Washington, USA

JOHN HUNT PUBLISHING

First published by Moon Books, 2022
Moon Books is an imprint of John Hunt Publishing Ltd., No. 3 East Street, Alresford
Hampshire SO24 9EE, UK
office@jhpbooks.net
www.johnhuntpublishing.com
www.moon-books.net

For distributor details and how to order please visit the 'Ordering' section on our website.

Text copyright: Lucya Starza 2021

ISBN: 978 1 78904 715 8
978 1 78904 716 5 (ebook)
Library of Congress Control Number: 2021930253

A CIP catalogue record for this book is available from the British Library.

Design: Matthew Greenfield

UK: Printed and bound by CPI Group (UK) Ltd, Croydon, CR0 4YY
Printed in North America by CPI GPS partners

We operate a distinctive and ethical publishing philosophy in
all areas of our business, from our global network of authors to
production and worldwide distribution.

Contents

Introduction

There's a chapter in Tolkien's *The Lord of the Rings* called 'The Mirror of Galadriel'. Frodo, the ringbearer, visits the Elven realm of Lothlorien where the Lady Galadriel invites him and his companions to join her in a magical glade by a stream to gain insight by looking for visions in water in a silver bowl. This is a form of scrying and here's the description:

> *Upon a low pedestal carved like a branching tree, stood a basin of silver, wide and shallow, and beside it stood a silver ewer.*
>
> *With water from the stream Galadriel filled the basin to the brim, and breathed on it, and when the water was still again she spoke. 'Here is the Mirror of Galadriel,' she said. 'I have brought you here so that you may look in it, if you will.'*
>
> *The air was very still, and the dell was dark, and the Elf-lady beside him was tall and pale. 'What shall we look for, and what shall we see?' asked Frodo, filled with awe.*
>
> *'Many things I can command the Mirror to reveal,' she answered, 'and to some I can show what they desire to see. But the Mirror will also show things unbidden, and those are often stranger and more profitable than things which we wish to behold. What you will see, if you leave the Mirror free to work, I cannot tell. For it shows things that were, and things that are, and things that yet may be. But which it is that he sees, even the wisest cannot always tell. Do you wish to look?'*

Although *The Lord of the Rings* is a work of fiction, the words of Galadriel are a good description of the way scrying using a mirror, crystal or vessel of water can work. You can ask questions, but you don't have to; you can just wait to see what is shown to you. What is revealed can indeed be the past, the present, or a possible future. It can be what you desire to see or something unbidden. The meaning of what you perceive might seem obvious, or obscure. Impressions are sometimes fleeting and essentially unrecordable and unprovable. It isn't the same as using tarot cards, where you can look up the meaning in a book. It is more like reading tea leaves or coffee grounds, although then you can photograph the shapes and patterns and study them at your leisure for as long as you like. In fact, tea-leaf and coffee-ground reading are so akin to more ephemeral forms of scrying that I've included a chapter on them. Scrying requires us to use our psychic senses and intuition to the full. But don't worry if that seems a tough task, this book will teach you how to do that. It's also okay to feel nervous at your first attempts. In *The Lord of the Rings* Frodo is reticent and doesn't initially answer the question posed to him by the Lady Galadriel about whether he wants to look into the magical mirror. His friend Sam, however, is curious and asks first to have a peep:

> *'I'd not mind a glimpse of what's going on at home,' he said in an aside to Frodo. 'It seems a terrible long time that I've been away. But there, like as not I'll only see stars, or something I won't understand.'*
> *'Like as not,' said the Lady with a gentle laugh. 'But come, you shall look and see what you may. Do not touch the water!'*
> *Sam climbed up on the foot of the pedestal and leaned over the basin. The water looked hard and dark. Stars were reflected in it.*
> *'There's only stars, as I thought,' he said. Then he gave a low gasp, for the stars went out. As if a dark veil had been withdrawn, the Mirror grew grey, and then clear...*

The Mirror of Galadriel does indeed show Sam, and the others, many things. As Galadriel said, *'things that were, and things that are, and things that yet may be.'* Note that she said *'may be'*, not *'will be'*. Like Galadriel in this fantastic tale, I don't believe the future is entirely fixed, or that things seen in any scrying device are necessarily true. Sometimes we see possible futures, sometimes we see things we hope will happen, or what we desire, but sometimes we see things we fear and sometimes we see a warning, enabling us to plan wisely for our own good or for the good of others. Often what we see offers insights about ourselves that may help us with the problems we face or what is yet to come. Do not act hastily after scrying. Make notes and think about what you've experienced; let the meaning of any visions become clearer with time. But we're getting ahead of ourselves; thinking about what to do after scrying. Before we even begin there's some background to understand and preparations to do...

Chapter 1

What is Scrying?

Before we get to the practical stuff, I'll delve a little into what scrying means and its origins. Scrying – sometimes just called 'seeing' – is looking into something in the hope of finding messages or visions. Often that's a reflective or dark surface, but not always. As well as crystal ball reading, it also means looking into bowls or pools of water, mirrors, flames, smoke, clouds, and a variety of other things too, including tea leaves or coffee grounds. It can be done for personal guidance, to find answers to questions, for inspiration, for far-seeing distant places or other realms, or for fortune-telling and prophecy. It's a form of divination that taps into our psychic senses and powers of intuition. This book shows how anyone can learn to develop the skill, although I should add the proviso that anyone with mental health concerns should talk to their GP or counsellor to check if it's suitable for them at that time. That goes for practising any type of magic or psychic work.

The word scry, meaning *'seeing images in crystal, water, etc, which reveal the future or secrets of the past'*, and *'to act as a crystal-gazer'*, is first recorded in writing in the early sixteenth century, according to the *Oxford English Dictionary*. The word was used earlier, but just meant *'catching sight of'* or *'viewing from afar'*. It fell out of popular use until the nineteenth century when crystal gazing became high fashion. However, the practice itself has been used in many cultures since ancient times, probably long before recorded history began. One can imagine the very earliest humans peering into pools of water or the embers of a fire and divining meanings from the patterns seen within.

Mirrors

The Ancient Egyptians believed what was reflected in a mirror had a life of its own. It was magical or even divine. An academic perspective by Barbara O'Neill in 'Reflections of Eternity: An Overview on Egyptian Mirrors from Prehistory to the New Kingdom', is that: *'The concept that the mirror actively 'saw', rather than simply reflected a living image, occurs early in Egypt.'* Of course, they used mirrors for mundane tasks such as putting on make-up as well as for magic, but the discs of polished metal they used had the reputation of showing more than a mere mirrored image. Pagan writer Cassandra Eason, in 'Mirror Scrying', relates the mythology associated with Hathor, perhaps the most ancient deity associated with mirror gazing and divination. The Ancient Egyptian Sky Goddess wears a disk representing the sun between a pair of horns on her head. As well as being a Goddess of joy and protector of women, she can see everything, including what lies in people's hearts. She has this ability by being able to look through the eye of her father, the Sun God Ra, as well as having a brightly polished shield that shows the true nature of all it reflects. According to tales, it was from this that the first magic mirror was formed. One side showed anywhere in the outer world the viewer desired to see, the other side gave them a true picture of themselves. Archaeologists have discovered two-sided metal mirrors, sometimes bronze, gold or copper on one side and silver on the other, in many Ancient Egyptian tombs. They often have long handles, some decorated with the face of Hathor. There's an example in London's Petrie Museum, along with Ancient Egyptian mirrors adorned with other motifs including lotus flowers. Others are in the collection of the British Museum and can be viewed online. These were often found in women's graves and were associated with that gender, although not exclusively.

Polished copper mirrors are also associated with Aphrodite, the Greek Goddess of Love, not just as a symbol of beauty and eroticism, but also as a tool for self-knowledge. Obsidian mirrors, as well as bowls of water, might have been used by the Aztecs and other Mesoamerican cultures for divination. The Aztec deity Tezcatlipoca's name is often translated as 'Smoking Mirror', which relates to the dark stone obsidian. In folklore, rituals that involve things like scrying include a tradition that young women gazing into a mirror in a darkened room could catch a glimpse of her future lover's face in a mirror after eating an apple.

Fictional accounts of magic mirrors abound, including the one I mentioned in my introduction, although Galadriel's magic mirror is a silver bowl filled with water. In Lewis Carroll's *Through the Looking-Glass*, Alice journeys to an imaginary realm where truths about the real world are highlighted by the symbolism of strange reversals. The most famous fictional magic mirror is in the fairy tale *Snow White*, where the jealous stepmother asks: '*Magic mirror on the wall / Who is the fairest of them all?*' That offers the message that we should be careful about the questions we ask, and whether we are ready to face any truths given in answer. Think before doing any psychic or magical work, and frame any words wisely.

Stone and Crystal Balls

Healers from the Yucatán Peninsula and Guatemala traditionally use stone balls known as sastun. Originally, they were Mayan antiquities from archaeological sites. Nowadays they're mostly modern. Jade balls have been found in ancient Mayan burials. Although we don't know for sure if they were used for scrying in ancient times, it's possible. In bygone centuries – even bygone millennia – scrying often meant finding out the will of the Gods, or learning the future through divine inspiration; that's the origin of the word 'divination'. It could involve studying patterns in natural objects with the idea that everything deities created contained the reflection of their will (as above, so below), but could include trying to converse with their messengers.

This was still true in medieval times. *'Medieval people longed to have conversations with angels,'* writes historian Sophie Page in *Spellbound: Magic, Ritual and Witchcraft.* While many practitioners used rituals found in grimoires, Sophie writes that a popular solution was to *'communicate through a medium that broke down the barriers between the physical and spirit worlds'* such as a crystal or mirror. These were believed to have the power to attract good spirits and trap evil spirits. The use of crystal balls wasn't new to medieval people. They have been found in pagan graves dating back to the fifth to seventh centuries, often those of female magical practitioners. By the eleventh to fifteenth centuries, crystal balls were sometimes placed in children's graves to protect them, as well as being aids for communication with spirits. Sophie writes:

> *This connection with the young and innocent was also reflected in the practice of skryers – virgin boys who acted as mediums for spirits drawn into the stone by the magical practitioner.*

Sixteenth-century occultist John Dee owned several crystals, which he and his colleague Edward Kelly used for scrying. Dee also owned an Aztec obsidian mirror. You can see his crystal ball and mirror in the British Museum in the Enlightenment Gallery, while London's Science Museum has a purple crystal that once belonged to him. Dee and Kelly are famous for their conversations with angels, primarily for the altruistic attainment of knowledge, although Dee's diaries also show him asking the whereabouts of hidden treasure.

Using crystal balls for scrying only became widely popular in the late nineteenth century, according to Professor Owen Davies in *Harry Potter: A History of Magic* (a superb book looking at the real history of magic behind that of JK Rowling's fictional wizardry). That's because mechanisation made it possible to produce crystal balls cheaply.

Bowls and Chalices

Tolkien's fictional Mirror of Galadriel being created by filling a bowl with water has plenty of basis in history and real-world mythology. The *Bible* mentions a silver chalice used by Joseph for both drinking and divination. *The Shahnameh*, a historical epic written in the tenth century, mentions the Cup of Jamshid from pre-Islamic Persia, used by magical practitioners for observing *'the seven layers of the universe'*. It was also said to contain an elixir of immortality, but it doesn't mention if this elixir helped with the scrying. If I ever find such an elixir, I'll certainly test its use in foretelling the future before deciding if that future is one in which I want to live forever. Nostradamus, the sixteenth-century astrologer and seer, would stare into a bowl of water or mirror to see the future while he was in trance. He is famous for his prophecies, many involving symbolism that's still open to interpretation.

Cunning Practices and Tea Leaves

Most of the examples from history and legend refer to wealthy or high-status people who could afford expensive crystals, mirrors or bowls of precious metal, or devices used by priests or priestesses or other specially appointed diviners in temples. Ordinary people scried as well, but the items they used were less remarkable. Those who worked as cunning folk or fortune tellers often got by perfectly well without them, using things readily to hand.

The first object I tried scrying with was a dark green fishing float owned by my parents. These were traditionally used as scrying balls by people living near the sea, especially in south-west England. My mother's family originally came from Cornwall. When I was a child, my family – mum, dad, grandma, me and any friends who were with us – would often do divination and fortune telling on Halloween and also on New Year's Eve; usually after an evening of party games. These are traditional times for fortune-telling. Most often we used playing cards, or a book my father owned called *The White Magic Book*, where you ask a question and then randomly turn to an answer within its pages, but sometimes we tried scrying with the fishing float. I have to say I never got good results back then, but that was probably because I was expecting too much and also because we were doing it in bright light. I'll go more into the ways to scry effectively in bright light, but it's not ideal.

Tea-leaf reading was another form of scrying used by nineteenth century and early twentieth century cunning folk and seers in England and Scotland. Tasseography or tasseomancy spread to Europe in the sixteenth century, when tea was introduced to the Western world. Techniques used by medieval European fortune-tellers who did readings from splatters of wax and lead got adapted. Tea was originally a very expensive drink in England. Coffee ground reading developed in places where Turkish coffee was drunk, as it leaves a thick sediment, although it is possible to read the grounds from cafetiere coffee too. Tea became a working-class drink in the nineteenth century, and coffee became more affordable in the twentieth century. The good thing is that all you need is loose-leaf tea or ground coffee, something to brew it in, and an ordinary cup. There are many traditions of how to interpret the symbols. The one I describe later on in this book is my own adaptation of methods popular in England and Scotland in relatively recent times.

How to Scry in a Dog's Bottom

I once saw a huge crystal ball on a stall at an antique market. As I was wondering if I could afford the equally huge price-tag, the stallholder said: *'It'd be even more expensive if it was a crystal ball that really worked.' 'It isn't the object that does the work, it's the person,'* I replied. *'I could scry into anything shiny.'* I picked up a black dog ornament on his stall and added: *'Even that dog's bottom.'* I later bought an ornament just like it, and I've since scried using it perfectly well.

While special devices might be essential for anyone following grimoire traditions or highly ceremonial religious or magical practices, most modern witches can scry without them just like our cunning folk ancestors would have done in the past. There's one form you can do without any special equipment at all; that's eyelid scrying. You just close your eyes and stare inside your eyelids. I've often done this myself, particularly when relaxing in a nice warm bath with the main lights turned off and the room lit by candlelight.

Exercise: Eyelid Scrying

All you need is to be in a safe, quiet place where you won't be disturbed, ideally somewhere dark or dimly lit. If you can't find anywhere that isn't brightly lit, put a scarf or sleep mask over your eyes to block out the light. Make sure you're sitting comfortably, or even lying down. Take a few deep breaths, in and out, then close your eyes, relax and look into your eyelids. I mean actually look, as though you are peering into the darkness. You might see nothing at first, or you might see the faint impressions caused by any exterior light viewed through your lids. Be patient and don't try to analyse anything you perceive, just be open to even tiny glimpses and let anything unfold naturally. You might notice vague shapes or shadows or colours or tiny lights, or you might start to get pictures or visions revealed either to your eyes or in your mind.

When you are ready to stop, open your eyes. Take a few more deep breaths, take off any eye-covering, blink a few times, turn on the lights or open the curtains and return to normality. That's a very basic method of scrying – although it doesn't go into interpretation yet. I hope it worked for you, but if it didn't, don't worry. This book will show you many ways to help your visions become clear, and cover interpreting them.

Your Book of Reflections

After any form of divination, even if you don't feel anything at all happened, it's always useful to make notes. You can use any notebook, your laptop, or even your phone, but if you're intending to scry regularly, it's ideal to keep a special journal. You could call it your Book of Reflections. After all, as well as meaning mirrored images, light or sound, reflection can mean contemplation – particularly in a spiritual sense. There's a chapter dedicated to this later, but for starters write down the date, time, place and phase of the moon if you know it. Make a note of the method you used, the length of the session and any other factors that seem important; particularly any issues that were on your mind at the time or any questions you asked. Jot down the impressions you got while scrying. If nothing at all happened, write that, but if you got even the tiniest of images or a thought popped into your head unbidden or you felt an emotion or sensation, that's something.

Grounding and Moving Forward

It's important to ground to bring yourself fully back to the everyday world after doing psychic or magical work, including scrying. Ideally have something to eat and drink, but if that isn't possible you can grip a surface tightly to feel its solidity or press or stamp your feet onto the floor. The following chapters go into more details about all aspects of scrying, from preparations through to grounding.

Chapter 2

Preparations for Scrying

However you choose to scry there are ways to make it more effective and preparation is key. Good preparation helps set the groundwork for success in a practical way, but going through a set ritual can also put you in the right frame of mind. I'll list the stages before going into each in more detail:

- Decide the focus for your scrying session
- Pick your time
- Set up your space
- Cleanse yourself, your space and your tools
- Use incense (optional)
- Get the lighting right
- Cast a circle
- Get comfortable and check your tools
- Get into the right mental state

Decide your Focus

Why are you scrying? Think about this first. It could be you have a specific question or an issue on your mind relating to any area of your life, including relationships, career or wellbeing. Try to formulate a question regarding this; one that doesn't just need a yes or no answer. For example, rather than asking whether you'll get a new job, ask: *'What will help me get a new job?'*, *'What factors are affecting my job applications?'*, or *'What would be the best type of job to apply for?'* You can scry for personal or spiritual self-development, to find an animal guide, for messages from the spirits of your ancestors or deities you honour. That narrows the focus. You don't absolutely have to have a specific question; you can just ask to see what the universe wants to show you.

Nevertheless, the narrower your focus and the more defined your question, the easier it will be to interpret whatever you experience. If you scry without any focus, it could take more effort to work out what you're being shown. Once you've settled on a question, write it down to refer to later. If you have a Book of Reflections, record it there.

Pick your Time

Picking the optimum time helps. The full moon, or the days leading up it or just afterwards, are often thought best for any magical or psychic work including scrying. Some witches find the new moon – when you can just see the first tiny crescent in the sky – is good for looking into the future. However, it's possible to scry at any phase of the moon, and if you have a burning question you aren't necessarily going to want to wait until the moon phase is perfect. You might be able to pick the best time of day. The liminal time of dusk, when day is turning into night, is when I find it easiest to do most kinds of magic. Some witches prefer to scry at night even when the moon isn't visible, while some prefer to scry just before dawn when the day is just being born and the world is full of possibilities. On a practical level, you might have to find a moment when you aren't busy with work, or when the kids are at school. Any time when you have peace and quiet and space to yourself will do. Experiment and find out what works best for you personally, as we are all different.

Set up your Space

Make sure you're in a safe place where you won't be disturbed; ideally somewhere as quiet and peaceful as possible. I'd recommend somewhere indoors to start with, as the environment's more controllable, but if you happen to have a private magical glade by all means go there and adapt these instructions to suit. If you do have a magical glade, I'm pretty envious by the way!

If you're new to magical or psychic work, then learning the best way to cleanse everything is important. Experienced witches reading this book will already know how to do ritual cleansing of sacred space and you can skip forward to the section on cleansing your scrying tools. Physically clean and tidy the room you'll be using. Be as thorough as your time and energy allow. Later you'll magical cleanse your space, but it's a good idea to run the vacuum cleaner round, put away random clutter and dust any table or altar for putting your tools on. You'll need something to sit on comfortably at the right height. Check how you'll adjust the lighting – closing the curtains and turning off electric lights for example – and make sure you have matches and candles in place if you're using them. Check the room temperature. You're likely to be sitting still for a time, so have something like a shawl or blanket to put on if you think you'll get cold.

Cleanse Yourself

It's good to be as physically clean as possible before doing any psychic or magical work. A shower is fine, but a ceremonial bath is even better to wash unwanted energy as well as unwanted grime from your body. Adding a little salt to your bath water will boost the effect, while scented oils or herbs can aid your intentions. You could use the herbs mentioned in 'Herbs for Cleansing' a little further on. If it isn't possible to have a bath or shower, then wash your face and hands as your senses of touch, sight, smell and hearing are what you'll be employing in the work to come.

Ritually Cleanse the Space

Witches perform cleansing rituals before most ceremonies, and it's useful before divination. Even if you've thoroughly dusted and vacuumed, ritual cleansing will get rid of unwanted energy so the intended magic isn't entangled with other thoughts and wishes that might be floating about. Here are some methods I use, with suggestions for those with mobility concerns:

Sweeping with a Broom

A besom is a traditional witches' broom and is used to clear space in many paths of English magic. You can buy traditional besoms at agricultural or country craft fairs and hardware or gardening shops, as they're also great for sweeping up dead leaves in the garden. You can even use a fancy-dress costume besom bought at Halloween, or an ordinary kitchen broom, if that's all you've got. It's the symbolism that counts. Go around the room in an anti-clockwise direction, sweeping from the centre outwards and visualising unwanted energy being swept away. The anti-clockwise (or widdershins) direction represents banishing.

Cleansing with Salt or Herbs in Water

Salt is an ancient cleansing product. It kills bacteria, but also has traditional uses in magical cleansing rites. Get a bowl of clean water and a pinch of salt. First, turn your attention to the water and visualise it being purified of unwanted energy. Then turn to the bowl of salt and dedicate it for your purpose of cleansing. Mix the salt and water, then sprinkle a little around your space. Alternatively use an infusion of cleansing herbs. Sprinkling with blessed or holy water is sometimes called 'asperging', which historically comes from the Latin word '*aspergo*' meaning 'to sprinkle'. Be careful not to get it on anything that could be damaged or stained. A twenty-first century alternative is to put salty water into a spray bottle for a fine mist.

Herbs for Cleansing

One herb commonly used – and which I've found works well – is mugwort (*Artemisia*). Dried mugwort can be ordered from pagan stores, but it grows wild in England. If you're picking it fresh, do so before it begins flowering, which it does from July to

September. This is a protective herb; it is reputed to keep harmful spirits at bay and promote psychic visions. As well as using it for sprinkling, you can burn it for smoke cleansing (see later). It's very mildly poisonous and so should be avoided by anyone who is pregnant. Some people say drinking a cup of mugwort infusion, or even just inhaling the vapours arising from it, greatly enhances divination. However, you should always check with a qualified herbalist before ingesting anything of that nature. If you are going to try it, make up two batches – one for cleaning and one for drinking!

Other herbs can be used for cleansing too. The various different types of sage, although different, are well known. White sage is often used for smoke cleansing. It's not native to Europe, so you might prefer to use a home-grown variety. Clary sage is often found as an essential oil, but can be used in a wash. You can use garden sage – which is native to Europe – in an infusion. Rosemary is another herb often used for cleansing rites.

Smoke Cleansing

Many traditions all over the world use smoke to purify sacred space. A general term for this is fumigation. Although that can also mean gassing pests, it traditionally meant using smoke for cleansing. The Native American ceremony of smudging uses a form of it. Spiritual smoke cleansing can be done by burning dried herbs on their own in a dish or in tightly bound bundles, or using mixed incense made from dried herbs, resins and tree bark. For incense, light a charcoal disk in a heatproof burner and sprinkle the mixture over the disk when it's glowing brightly, then allow the smoke to fill all the space to be cleansed. You can waft it into corners using a fan or just your hand. Put incense burners on things that won't get damaged by heat. Incense can also be used for its properties in helping with psychic work. I'll go into that in more details later. A simpler and cheaper alternative is to use incense sticks.

Cleansing with Light

I love using light to cleanse space. While I often open up the curtains and let sunlight flood into my room then visualise it chasing away all unwanted energy, that doesn't set the right mood when I'm dimming the lights to prepare for scrying. Also, some people prefer not to let daylight touch any of the objects they use for scrying. Sunlight can fade some crystals and dyes, and can also be concentrated by crystal balls to start a fire. You might want to cover your crystals with a dark cloth before you let sunlight into your sacred space. If the moon is in the sky, you can cleanse by moonlight. You can also carry a candle around, especially into dark corners where natural light doesn't reach. Put the candle securely in a lantern or jar first as you don't want it to fall over and set light to anything. A safer alternative is to leave the candle on a flat surface, then use a wand and visualise spreading the light all around you.

Cleanse your Tools

The first time you use a scrying device, or if it's been handled by others, you should cleanse it of unwanted energy. That generally just means thoughts and emotions that might have become attached to it. I also always cleanse scrying tools before using them to make sure they're as physically clean as possible, not grubby and smeary. You can rinse most solid objects in slightly salty water and then running water, or you can cleanse them in a herbal infusion. I usually use mugwort. If you asperged with an infusion to cleanse the room, you can use that to clean your crystal ball or mirror. Unlike in *The Wizard of Oz*, witches don't dissolve in water, but obviously anything made of paper or card shouldn't be soaked. Some crystals are also water soluble, so be careful. Quartz, amethyst and obsidian are safe in room-temperature water, while fluorite, selenite, opal, and hematite should be kept dry. If you buy a crystal, always ask whether it is safe to wash in pure water and salty water, as salt can be a bit corrosive. Although you can fumigate scrying devices or cleanse them with light, this won't make them physically clean and shiny. While you need to cleanse unwanted energy from the object, you also want to get rid of greasy smudges that will affect your viewing. Polishing with a cloth is an alternative to washing. If you're eyelid scrying, give your face a special rinse in a cool infusion.

Exercise: Cleansing

Cleanse all your scrying devices, including crystal balls, mirrors, glasses and bowls, then dry them if necessary and polish them with a clean cloth. Even if you're not immediately using them for a scrying session, it's a good idea to cleanse them regularly.

Using Incense

Burning incense can help you get into the right state of mind. Use it if it helps you and is allowed where you are, but it isn't essential and if it makes you cough or your eyes water, then it's going to be a distraction. If it's likely to set the fire alarm off and you don't fancy a bunch of burly fire-fighters bursting through your door, give it a miss. You can use loose incense on charcoal, cones, sticks, oils in an oil diffuser, or even a scented candle. Really, use whichever you prefer. Loose incense on charcoal has a ceremonial feel, but is more work than cones or sticks. If you buy cones or sticks made with real herbs and resins rather than artificial perfumes then they're pretty much as good. Oils in a diffuser or scented candles will minimise smoke, but some oils can be harmful to animals so check or keep your pets out of the room.

You can make your own incense. I've already mentioned mugwort as being protective, keeping harmful spirits at bay and promoting visions and other psychic work. It can be used in incense as well as for cleansing washes. Here are some herbs you can use in incense in scrying sessions, mixed with mugwort or other herbs, or on their own:

Wormwood

This is protective and boosts psychic powers. It's in the same family of plants as mugwort and in fact sometimes the names mugwort and wormwood are used synonymously. Wormwood is a bitter herb used to make the alcoholic drink absinthe. Burnt in incense with sandalwood, wormwood is traditionally used to help communication with spirits. Again, it's a bit poisonous. *Cunningham's Book of Shadows* suggests equal parts of mugwort and wormwood as a recipe for a scrying incense to be burnt on charcoal.

Sandalwood

Sandalwood is one of my favourite types of incense. It's protective and boosts magical endeavours. However, sandalwood trees have a vulnerable conservation status, so make sure anything you buy is sourced ethically.

Lavender

I'm mentioning this because I think it's good to know what common herbs you can use. Lavender is a cleansing and purifying herb. It promotes positive thoughts and is also connected to divination. As well as being good in scrying incense mixes, you can put a little lavender into a pillow to sleep on to encourage divinatory dreams. Lavender oil in a diffuser can scent the room while scrying if you don't like smoke.

Get the Lighting Right

In my experience, crystal ball gazing, mirror reading and the like are best done by candlelight or moonlight. The moon is associated with powers of divination, but why candlelight? Well, candles create a magical type of lighting. Most witchcraft rituals that take place after dark do so by candlelight. The soft glow helps mentally transport us outside normal space and time to a liminal place where all things are possible – the best place for magic to work. That's reason enough to use candlelight for scrying. Another practical reason is that very low light levels are conducive for getting results when crystal ball gazing or similar. You see too much of the normal world reflected if you do it in bright light. It's possible to scry in bright lights, but it's more difficult in my experience. There's more about scrying in daylight in a later chapter.

The reflection of candlelight in a crystal or glass can be used to help get into the right state of mind for scrying – a light trance. Generally, I make my room as dark as possible then light a candle and place it next to my scrying device or behind it, and often slightly above it. I tend to use a pillar candle, dinner-table candle or a tealight in a tall holder as that produces the best results for me. Some prefer lights lower down, especially if they're using a crystal ball, but everyone's different. Experiment to get the lighting perfect for yourself. You can have a second candle if you want a bit of extra light, perhaps one candle on your altar and another to illuminate your crystal ball, cauldron or mirror. Some psychics using mirrors like to place one each side. Some use three candles set around their device and find that gives them a better effect.

Cast a Circle

When I'm doing spells or rituals, I usually cast a circle as a safe and sacred place within which to work magic. You can scry without a circle, but it's a good psychic safety measure. If you're an experienced witch then you'll have your own way of circle casting and can skip to 'Get Comfortable', but if you don't know how to cast one, here are simple instructions.

Circles are intended to keep out unwanted or potentially negative influences – and you don't want anything negative interrupting you when you're scrying. A circle won't keep out your kids or pets, so close the door as well if necessary. Most witches use a wand, athame or pointed finger to cast a circle.

They walk around the perimeter, pointing their pointy thing, and visualising drawing a protective circle around themselves in energy. Sometimes they ask the elements and spirit or deities to guard their circle too, but you don't have to. If you aren't very mobile or are in a small space, you can just sit still and visualise a globe of protective light spreading out all around you. Personally, I like to cast my circle using a candle. Starting in the northernmost edge of my space, I go around in a clockwise, or deosil, direction with a lit candle in a suitable holder. I visualise the light creating an invisible barrier that stretches up over my head and down under my feet in a globe all around the space. Then I put the candle down where it can serve as my scrying light or on my altar. Whatever way you cast your circle, here are some words you can say:

I cast this circle to be a safe and sacred space in which to scry. May it protect and guard me on this night. So mote it be.

If you cast your circle with a candle, it not only gives extra light, but also indicates the continued presence of your circle of protection.

Get Comfortable

It's really important to be safe and comfortable while you're scrying. Right at the start of preparation, you checked you had a suitable chair and a table or altar with all you needed, but check once more that everything's in the right place, at the right height, and is safe and secure. Make sure you are comfortable. Then you can begin to get into the right mental state.

The Right State of Mind

Before starting any spells or scrying, I spend a little time meditating to calm myself and put aside intrusive thoughts. This is particularly important for scrying, because you need to get into the right frame of mind. Meditation is perfect as a prelude to the light trance state required. You can use a candle flame as the focus. As with most types of meditation, you need to be in a restful position, usually seated. Ideally have the candle at eye height, although that isn't always possible if you're using a tealight. Make sure it's securely in its holder. Take a few deep breaths in and out while gazing on the flame. As you breathe in visualise breathing in light from the candle; as you breathe out visualise all stresses and worries leaving your body. Do this at least three times until you start to feel calm and at ease.

You can also use a bowl of water, perhaps mixed with salt or herbs, to get into the right mental state. Gaze into the bowl of water or stir the water gently with your finger and visualise your unwanted thoughts, fears, worries, and mundane concerns dissolving into it. You can use the same bowl you used to clear your space. Don't pour your unwanted thoughts into water you're later going to scry into though!

Trance States

After you've meditated and minimised unwanted thoughts, you need to get your mind into a light trance state – like being on the very edge of sleep. The scrying medium you're going to use, whether that's a crystal ball, mirror or a bowl of water or whatever, can help focus your attention to get into a slightly hypnotic state. Candlelight or moonlight, rather than full daylight or bright electric lights, also help. Use the exercise below a few times. When you've practised getting into the right mental state of a light trance, you're ready to start scrying...

Exercise: Trance Practise

For this exercise you need a scrying device, which could be a bowl or glass of water, but could also be a crystal or glass ball, a dark mirror, or just a regular hand-held mirror. You will also need to be somewhere you won't be disturbed for at least five minutes. If you have a timer, you can set it for three minutes before you start, but that's not essential.

Dim the lights. Get comfortable, and hold your scrying device in your hands. Take a few slow, regular breaths. Relax. With half-closed eyes gaze into your device, whatever it is, or across its surface. Don't yet try to look for messages or visions; just look at the sparkles in the polished mirror or crystal or surface of the water. Let those sparkles entrance you. Look within. Let your mind become clear. If you are using a dark object, gaze into that darkness without looking for anything there at all. Let the edges of that darkness softly and gently envelop you. You can also gaze into the shadows within a crystal ball. Remember to breathe slowly, in and out, in and out, in and out. Do this for about three minutes. However, don't look at the clock or your phone to check; keep your attention gently on the ball, mirror or water.

When you feel your three minutes is up, or when you feel you need to stop, take a deep breath and look away from the device. Put it down, shake your fingers and toes and return to normal consciousness. Check the time – was it about three minutes? Time can seem to move very differently when you're in a trance state, but that's okay. When you feel you have practised getting into a light trance successfully, you can move on to the next chapter.

Chapter 3

How to Scry

Now you've prepared everything and practised getting into a light trance, you can begin to scry. Images or other psychic messages might come to you as soon as you start, but if they don't, this chapter offers ways of making it work. First of all, it can take time. That's absolutely fine. The most important thing is not to fret about it. Everyone's different and it isn't a race to get the first vision or a competition to see the most things. Quality is more important than quantity. A single insight that helps you is worth a dozen readings that make no difference to your life. When I first began scrying it often took some time for me to experience anything at all, and sometimes I saw nothing. The reason I teach scrying is because it took me a while to learn to do it myself, and I firmly believe anyone can train themselves to scry with enough time and practise. Nowadays, I generally see things quickly and I feel that if I could learn the skill, anyone can, and I enjoy passing on the tips I've learnt over the years.

It always helps to relax and it's often good to defocus the eyes slightly – I usually half close my eyelids. Beyond that, there are two common techniques for scrying. The first is to use the device as though it's a window. You look into it or through it rather than staring at the surface. The second is to gaze at the light reflected off the surface instead of looking into it. They might seem a bit contradictory, but I would suggest trying both and seeing which works best for you. Be patient. If you have a question, picture it in your mind. If you don't have a specific question, it still helps to ask your scrying device to work for you. I sometimes use the following words:

Crystal ball in front of me,
Show me what I need to see

Obviously if you are using a dark mirror, silver bowl or candle flame, use those words instead of 'crystal ball'. If you work with elementals, you can ask the element associated with your device – air, fire, water or earth – to help you. Likewise, you can call on deities or spirits you normally work with, but that isn't essential as scrying is primarily an intuitive or psychic skill. Then, try to keep a relaxed state of mind. As I said earlier, ideally your state of mind should be like the slightly hypnotic state everyone enters just before sleep – but do try not to actually nod off if you can help it. You don't want to be woken when your face meets a very solid crystal or bowl of cold water!

Some people report feeling sensations in their foreheads or between their eyes just before their psychic senses start working. It can be a tightness or an itching. I sometimes get a slightly swirly sensation, but you might not feel anything. Some people find the crystal or mirror starts to cloud or fog over and then comes back into focus sharply just before any impressions begin. If that doesn't happen for you, don't worry. We're all different.

What to Look For

When I first had a go at scrying, I was still a child and I expected to see a sort of movie displayed in the glass fishing float. I was disappointed when that didn't materialise. I thought I was doing it wrong or didn't have the talent. Actually, not everyone gets that sort of film-like display – or at least not always or not at first – although some do. There are various different recognised forms of psychic perception you might find when you scry. There's no right or wrong way and it's good to be open to messages coming in all sorts of styles.

- Clairvoyance: Seeing. This can be clear images in the crystal or beyond it, or it can be vague shapes or symbols or just flashes of colour or it could be pictures in your mind's eye.
- Clairaudience: Hearing. You might hear voices or other sounds.
- Clairsentience: Sensing/feeling. Perhaps you sense an emotion, feel hot or cold or feel something brush against your skin.
- Clairalience: Smelling. Technically I would classify smelling as part of clairsentience, but sometimes it has its own name. Smells can be very evocative. Sometimes people say they smell lavender when a spirit or ghost is present, although when the ghost of the long-departed yet still nosey high priestess who trained me in witchcraft decides to pop in to give me a message, I sometimes smell the cigarettes she loved to smoke.
- Claircognizance: Just knowing. This is probably the most difficult to describe, but sometimes when you are scrying you just know something is true. It is a weird kind of certainty without knowing why you are certain, but of course it is easy to mistake your own wishful thinking for claircognizance so do check things out carefully afterwards. If you struggle with visualising images, you can still get psychic impressions with claircognizance.

These are all valid. I would also add that sometimes you become aware of a material aspect of the scrying device or the room that seems significant to you. Sometimes you will be aware of pareidolia. That's the word for when we see faces in trees, butterflies in inkblots, or clouds in our coffee, when in fact it is our mind making out a pattern from random shapes. When you are scrying, don't dismiss pareidolia as being just an illusion. It can be your intuition using flaws in the crystal to make you think of something relevant to your question. Sometimes words might pop into your head rather than pictures. These can also be your intuition at work.

On the other hand, you might feel what you are getting is a message from spirit or from a deity. This is particularly likely if you honour or work with a specific God, Goddess or ancestor in your regular spiritual or magical practice, and if you have asked them for help and guidance. Sometimes what you sense is symbolic, like dream imagery, rather than having a clear and specific meaning. Don't try to over-analyse things while you're scrying, just mentally note them. Some psychics like to say out loud what they see. You can have a recording device working if you do this, but obviously not in a room with other people who are also scrying as it will distract them. Have your Book of Reflections and pen ready to write things down. It's best to wait until after you've finished, as stopping to write can break your concentration, but sometimes you might feel you need to interrupt the session to record something important before you forget it. If so, don't change the light levels, and return to scrying as soon as possible. If absolutely nothing is happening at all, try breathing slowly and deeply in and out again, and focus on the centre of the scrying device with half-closed lids. Cassandra Eason in *Scrying the Secrets of the Future*, suggests:

> *Look into the scrying medium and picture a small pure white dot in the center that grows slowly into a sphere of light that covers a third of the inside or surface.*

When you've done that, see if you can see anything in that circle. Try observing the light reflected off the surface of the device, or cast your eye around the interior or edges of the ball, mirror or cauldron as sometimes things will first be seen at the edges rather than the centre.

If you're working with a black mirror or ball, then look into the very darkest part to see if anything emerges. You can empty your mind while gazing with slightly unfocused eyes and try not to force things. Sometimes, if you are not getting anything from one position, a change can make all the difference. With bowls or cauldrons of water, some witches will swirl the cold liquid with a finger and look for shapes in the patterns. They might also fan smoke from incense, or breathe onto the device three times. It's perfectly acceptable to move your scrying tools or pick them up if that's practical. Sometimes the sense of touch will spark your intuition. You can move your candle so the light shines from a better position, so long as it is safe to move. Obviously don't touch anything that's hot though. Some people find passing their hands over the device can help. You can visualise empowering it as you do so. In *Pagan Portals: Divination*, Melusine Draco writes:

> *Frequent passes made with the right hand give power to the crystal, and those made with the left hand give it sensitivity which, when the eyes of the gazer look into it, becomes a medium.*

If at any time during the scrying session something happens that makes you feel uncomfortable or which you find scary and don't want to contemplate, then in your mind say: *'Leave this crystal (or cauldron or whatever), go in peace, be gone.'* Hopefully that will move on the thing you didn't want to see. If it doesn't, you can end the scrying session a bit earlier than you otherwise intended. There's more about dealing with scary stuff later in the book.

End the Scrying Session

When you are ready to stop scrying, mentally say to yourself: *'I am now ending this scrying session.'* If you feel you have had contact from any spirits or guides, thank them and say goodbye to them. Blink your eyes a few times. It can help to have a little shake of your body and wiggle your fingers and toes.

Open the Circle

When you've finished doing any magic you should thank any elementals, deities or spirits you worked with, then ask them to leave. If you cast a circle, take it down. That's sometimes called opening the circle. The way I do it is to walk around the edge in a widdershins (anticlockwise) direction and visualise the energy withdrawing back into my candle. If you use a wand, direct the energy into the ground. You can just sit in the centre and visualise the circle opening. Say: 'The circle is open.' Then turn on any main lights and extinguish your candles.

Exercise: Scrying

Yes, have a go. It doesn't matter what device you use. If you don't own a crystal ball, dark mirror or cauldron, then find a bowl, pan or cup in the kitchen. Half-fill it with water and use that for your first attempt at this exercise. Allow yourself about 15 to 20 minutes for a first attempt – you can set a timer if you want to. However, if you need to end the scrying session earlier than that, then do so, that's okay. While you are scrying, ask yourself:

'What am I seeing?'
'What am I hearing?'
'What am I sensing?'
'What am I feeling?'
'What am I becoming aware of?'
'What is becoming clearer?'

Repeat these questions to yourself as often as you need. After you have finished scrying, make notes and don't forget to ground properly. There's more on those things in the next chapter.

Chapter 4

Journaling and Grounding

Your Book of Reflections

After scrying, make notes of everything that came to you in the session, which you can compare to any question or focus you recorded before you began. As I mentioned earlier, you can call your journal your Book of Reflections. If you have more than one scrying device, note which you used. What you saw might make complete sense to you immediately, but the chances are it'll need interpreting. Images are often dreamlike, symbolic, allegorical or just unclear. It isn't like using tarot, where you can look up the official meaning of a card in a book. What we see when we scry is usually highly personal to us, as it's filtered through our own perceptions and the device we're using. It doesn't matter if it seems irrelevant, it might turn out to be significant. If you take good notes at the time, you can read over them later to try to work out what they might mean. At the end of this book there's a chapter called 'Interpreting Shapes and Symbols', which offers more help with working out the meanings of what you've experienced; this section's more about taking good notes.

I'd also recommend recording the date, the time you started and ended, the phase of the moon and anything else that's important or feels relevant. That could be how you were feeling beforehand, events that had happened and anything else on your mind. I often record the weather conditions, the light level in the room, and the temperature. I sometimes sketch things I've seen even though I'm no great artist. What you choose to record is completely up to you, but here's one entry from my own Book of Reflections:

October 2ⁿᵈ, 2020.

Moon: 99.5% waning gibbous (just past full).

Mood before: Feeling irritable as my boiler had stopped working and the house was cold.

Device used: Clear glass ball on black velvet beanbag.

Light levels: Candlelight in room with closed curtains.

Other factors: Weather outside cloudy, promising rain.

Focus: 'Crystal ball in front of me, show me what I need to see.'

Time started: 2.40pm.

I see an owl flying straight at me. The owl looks at me; I feel fearful. 'Can I ask a question?' 'No,' I sense. 'It is important to face fears.' The owl changes into a dragon. It faces me. It is staring at me. I see its eyes glowing and its teeth. I feel fear again. 'Do not fear,' I sense as a message. I continue looking. We look into each other's eyes. The fear goes. Beyond the fear is love, and joy, and passion. It is important to look beyond fear.

Time ended: 3pm

If you scry regularly you will probably start to notice repeating images. By keeping regular notes of everything you see, you can look back and spot symbols that recur. They could have more ongoing significance for you than things you notice just once. I often see owls. In fact, I often see owls when I'm doing guided visualisations too. I regard them as bringers of messages. For anyone who enjoys the *Harry Potter* books, owls might also symbolise that – although I've felt owls were bringers of messages from the subconscious since before I read that series. When I was a child, an owl rested in a hollow high up in a tree at the end of my garden during the day. I used to love to see it there, unmoving but magnificent. Every evening at dusk it would swoop down over the lawn, and I would often watch for it out of an upstairs window in my house. In the morning, the bird of prey would be back in its tree, but I would find dry owl pellets in the garden. Sometimes I would pull them apart to try to work out what the owl had hunted that night, and imagine what it did while I was fast asleep.

Owls can mean many things to many people. In traditional English folklore, they were often considered bad luck, even harbingers of death, but they can also represent witchcraft, the night and mysteries, as well as being sacred to the Goddess of Wisdom, Athena. The Welsh Goddess Blodeuwedd was turned into an owl as a supposed punishment for her independence of mind, as anyone who has read Alan Garner's *The Owl Service* or is familiar with Welsh mythology will know. They have sharp eyesight, and can see in very low light to spot anything they're looking for, so are perfect symbols for anyone scrying.

Grounding

When you've finished scrying and taking notes, it's vital to ground. That means bringing yourself totally back down to earth and getting rid of any lingering energies from the session. Personally, I find the best way to do that is to have something to eat and drink. Salty food is very grounding, so I often pass around a little salty popcorn at my workshops, but at home I have tea and biccies (that's cookies to Americans). Obviously avoid any food you're allergic to. If you don't have anything to eat or drink available you can tap the table three times with your hand, or stamp your feet on the floor if you prefer. Some witches use visualisation techniques for grounding, but I find physical activity is better for connecting with the real world after psychic or magical work.

Exercise: Reviewing your Book of Reflections

After you've grounded and tidied away the objects you were scrying with, open up your Book of Reflections again and reread what you recorded in your session. Think about what it means.

If it isn't completely obvious to you, then on a separate piece of paper write down all the main points as list headings. Under each heading, brainstorm everything you can think of that might relate to it. Then, consider how each of those interpretations feels to you. Use your intuition – if it feels completely unconnected then it probably is. If it feels it might be connected, then it's worth looking at further. Make more notes in your Book of Reflections about how you are starting to analyse your visions.

Over the next few days and nights, be aware of things that happen or dreams you have that might be related to what you saw. Note them in your Book of Reflections too. Make a point of opening your notebook regularly and reviewing your initial experiences, your analysis, and your experiences. If you need extra prompting use the chapter in this book on interpreting symbols, but don't make that your first port of call.

Chapter 5

Tools of the Craft

Now I'm going to take a more in-depth look at the tools of the craft. While I've already said you can scry into pretty much anything – even a pottery dog ornament – some objects are more conducive to getting results than others. I'm not ruling out the idea that a few scrying devices are in themselves inherently magical, or house spirits that conduct messages, but most crystal balls you will buy are just crystal balls. Nevertheless, the material they're made of can have qualities that will help you. As I mentioned earlier, things used in scrying often have reflective, refractive, translucent, or luminescent surfaces, particularly crystals, glass, polished metal, smooth dark surfaces and water.

Crystal Balls and Dark Mirrors

The term scrying is often seen as synonymous with gazing into crystal balls, sometimes called crystallomancy or spheromancy, or obsidian mirrors, technically called catoptromancy. It's hard to shake the common idea that they're the best tools for the job, and that anything else is second or third best. There are reasons why crystals are conducive to good results. Partly that's because of the properties associated with them. I'll go into the characteristics of various crystals often used for scrying, but if you're going to buy them new, make sure they come from an ethical source. Too many are mined in ways that are destructive to the environment or by workers in appalling conditions.

Quartz

The most common crystal used for spheres these days is quartz. It's the most versatile crystal for psychic, magical or healing use and isn't particularly expensive. You can use quartz to boost the power of any magical working. It amplifies your psychic abilities, is great for communication spells and perfect for scrying. Clear quartz is found worldwide. Clear, colourless quartz is known as rock crystal. Some polished spheres are made of that. You can also get quartz balls with inclusions that look like fine hairs or needles. They are caused by crystallised minerals that were enclosed by the growing quartz crystals. You also get milky quartz with whitish patterns like clouds inside. That's caused by tiny amounts of fluid being encased in the crystal when it formed. Smoky quartz is also popular for scrying. It usually has blackish or smoky grey hues, although sometimes slightly brown or yellow. John Dee's crystal ball is a clear smoky quartz. If you want the science, the smoky colour comes from free silicon formed from the silicon dioxide by natural irradiation. It's good for grounding, but is also calming, encourages a positive attitude and is used for healing in general. It helps with meditation and in scrying can help you get into the right frame of mind, give clear insight, promote concentration and help you get over fears of failure. There's mixed opinions on whether perfectly clear crystal balls or ones with imperfections are best for scrying. It really depends on the technique you tend to use and personal preference.

Amethyst

Amethyst is a traditionally thought of as protective. It guards against unwanted energy or psychic influence, enhances higher states of consciousness and helps meditation. It can boost intuition and other psychic powers. Amethyst is good for cleansing unwanted energy too. For these reasons it can be good as a scrying ball, although another suggestion is to put a small amethyst at the base of your device to protect, cleanse and boost your efforts. If you make a beanbag stand for a crystal ball, you could pop a tiny amethyst or two into it. Some people find crystal ball reading makes them feel a little headachy, and many say having an amethyst to hand helps avoid that. However, if you often get headaches do see your doctor or optician in case you need medical help or a new pair of glasses.

Beryl

Beryl was a popular stone for divination in the Middle Ages. Sometimes it was thrown into a bowl of water and the ripples read. Sometimes it was done through dowsing: attaching the beryl to string and holding it over a bowl of water. The bowl was marked with letters, and the pendulum could work in a similar way to a Ouija board. Some books on scrying say the first crystal balls were made of beryl before clear quartz became popular, but this was probably a corruption of the low Latin word for magnifying glass, beryllus, and might have been used for anything clear that helped people see, even polished glass. Some beryl is clear – although it is most often coloured blue or green by impurities. White beryl is associated with clear thinking and truth as well as stress reduction, so it is suitable for scrying.

Glass

Many inexpensive scrying balls are made of glass or even plastic – and these are alternatives if you prefer to avoid buying crystals these days. Some high-quality glass is actually called 'crystal', which means it has a high lead content. That makes it very sparkly. Some psychics say the lead is good for grounding, while the sparkliness helps achieve a trance-like state easily. You can use glass fishing floats and glass paperweights too – they're pretty traditional.

Obsidian

This has traditionally been used for dark mirrors. It is molten lava that didn't have time to crystallise, so can be naturally smooth and shiny as well as black in colour. It's protective, but it also helps us see the unknown and look past blockages that are preventing us from realising things we need to understand but perhaps find difficult to face. That's possibly one of the reasons it has a reputation for showing things that are scary, although horror films have no doubt added fictional fears to the legends. It's a powerful stone, but can be really good for scrying, so use it if you feel drawn to do so. You can also put a small piece of obsidian next to another scrying device, or put one into a bowl of water to help with your scrying if you don't have an actual obsidian mirror.

Other Crystals and Alternatives

Other crystals can be used for their magical associations. Examples include citrine for questions about wealth, health and success; rose quartz for love questions; and agates for balancing all sides of a situation before making a decision. Expensive items aren't necessarily going to be best for everyone. Personally, I scry best with a plain glass ball I picked up at a charity shop attached to a tacky ornamental elephant. As much as I like real elephants, the plastic pachyderm went to the recycling and the large glass ball got a new home on a black velvet cushion. My recommendation is to try out cheap options before spending money on an expensive crystal.

While an obsidian mirror might be top notch, a piece of glass painted black on the reverse can be used adequately. Cecil Williamson's dark mirror in the Museum of Witchcraft and Magic is glass backed with either dark paint or dark fabric (I was going to say 'dark material', but that has esoteric connotations and I wanted to point out it was pretty mundane in the way it was made). Doreen Valiente in *An ABC of Witchcraft* offers a way of making your own black mirror. You need a round, concave piece of glass – like the glass from the front of an old clock – and some black paint. Put three coats of black paint on the convex or upward-curving side of the glass, ideally while the moon is waxing. That will give it a good covering. Doreen Valiente then writes that you should consecrate the mirror under the full moon. To consecrate it you can simply clean it with mugwort, let moonlight shine on the surface, then ask the moon to help and guide you when you scry. After that, the instructions are that you should never let sunlight fall on it again. Mind you, if you do, I would say just reconsecrate it and be more careful in future. I've made dark mirrors that way and it does work extremely well. I've also made a black scrying ball by painting the inside of a spherical bottle with black paint.

What to Put your Balls On

Crystal balls, not anything saucy... There are lots of traditions regarding the best thing to rest your scrying devices on. You obviously need to stop spheres rolling off the table and smashing on the floor, but the bottoms of flat objects like mirrors still need protecting from scratches. Stands, cushions and mats for scrying devices also serve other purposes – both practical and magical. Ebony is one of the traditional things to use for a crystal ball stand. It's a very hard, black wood. It's protective and boosts psychic and magical power, as well as being associated with all the five elements, so is balancing. Ebony stands are lovely and really look the part too – but it is a rare and endangered wood and trade in it is illegal in some countries. It really isn't essential to use it.

Another traditional thing to place your scrying device on is black silk. I've made small black fabric beanbags, which I think work well as they cradle the crystal nicely. You could add a few tiny pieces of ebony – or jet, which is fossilised wood – to a beanbag, or you can add amethyst or quartz crystals, or dried herbs. Many diviners use black cloth of some kind to rest their scrying device on, or to wrap around it to stop reflections while they're using it. The same cloth can be put over it when it's not in use. While silk is traditional, I've used other black materials – including velvet – perfectly adequately. In the picture on the cover of this book you'll see one of my quartz balls on a metal stand. You can buy others made of resin, glass and various kinds of wood. The most important thing really is that it holds the ball securely at a good height, and you are happy with it.

Exercise: Make a Scrying Beanbag

You need some black fabric (velvet is ideal), needle and thread, and dried beans or dried rice. Cut two circles of black fabric using a saucer or small plate as a template. With the right sides facing, stitch a seam around most of the edge, leaving a little gap unstitched. Turn the stitched circles right side out. Put enough dried rice or beans inside to make a beanbag things can rest on. You can also add small crystals or dried herbs if you want. Neatly stitch the remaining gap to close it up. Use your little beanbag cushion to put your scrying device on.

Keep Grounded and Protected

Jet jewellery – particularly a necklace – is good to wear if you are scrying as it is grounding. It's called the witches' stone, although it is actually fossilised wood. It absorbs negative energy and if you find psychic work tends to give you a headache – it does with some people – wearing jet can help prevent that. As I've mentioned earlier, see your GP if you often get headaches. Another witches' stone is amber, which is fossilised resin. It helps you tap into your magical potential. Some witches wear necklaces made of amber alone or amber and jet. Another protective stone is one found with a natural hole in it. These are often called hagstones and were traditionally hung up in homes to protect them from malignant energy. If you find one of them on a beach where beachcombing is permitted, you could put it next to you or wear it for protection when you scry.

Storing Crystals and Mirrors

Some people say you should never let sunlight fall onto your crystal ball or dark mirror. The practical reasons are that light can fade or damage crystals, and crystal spheres can focus sunbeams and cause fires. Magically, the theory is that if you have a device attuned to moonlight, you should only use it in that kind of light. I'm not exceptionally scrupulous, but I do cover my own crystal balls with a dark cloth when not in use and I store my scrying mirror in a velvet bag.

Another area of divided opinion is whether you should let anyone else touch your divination tools. Many traditional and modern witches believe that you shouldn't let anyone else handle them once you've dedicated them for your personal use. Melusine Draco, in *Pagan Portals: Divination*, writes: *'The crystal should never be handled by anyone but its owner.'* Tradition is a powerful aid to magic, but I have to say I've let many people use my crystal balls and dark mirrors. I regularly run scrying workshops and I can't afford to keep one set for my students and another set for myself. When I've been part of a coven, I've happily let my sisters in the craft scry alongside me and I've even lent them my magical tools. I've also bought plenty of second-hand items in the past. I always thoroughly cleanse an item after someone else has used it and I don't let people handle things who aren't respectful of their purpose. However, as with most things magical, do what you feel is best for you. Belief and tradition are powerful aids to all aspects of witchcraft. Those who like to test things could run an experiment: get two identical crystal balls. Keep one untouched by anyone except yourself but let your fellow witches share the other one. Put a tiny mark on each to tell them apart but cover them so you can't see the marks. Mix them up and try scrying with both to see if you notice a difference in your results or can guess which is which. Then uncover the marks and see if you were right.

Cauldrons and Bowls

After crystals, scrying into bowls of water is probably the best-known method. Cauldrons are ideally witchy. They are one of the most traditional tools associated with the craft. Shakespeare's play *Macbeth*, from the early seventeenth century, portrays weird sisters in a cavern, standing around a boiling cauldron. They offer predictions to the would-be king of Scotland by summoning apparitions in the steam above their bubbling brew. The 1620 engraving 'The Witches' Sabbath', by Michael Herr, shows a cauldron surrounded by cavorting figures. A cauldron also stands in the centre of the picture 'The Magic Circle' by John William Waterhouse, from 1886. Cauldrons have heaps of magical symbolism. Before we had stoves in our kitchens, cauldrons suspended over open fires were a main means of cooking. Women would have used the tools available to them, including cauldrons and broomsticks, for magic as well as household chores. The cauldron represents feminine arts and is womblike in that things are created and transformed within it. Being dark inside it also represents a receptacle for things unconscious or hidden. When scrying, it is those unconscious or hidden things we most want to see.

Scrying into steam might have made a better picture or look better on a stage, but nowadays most witches tend to scry into cold water or herbal infusions inside a cauldron rather than look for visions in vapours rising above a vessel over a fire. It's more practical. Seeing as most modern kitchens don't have cauldrons among the regular cooking pots, how do you go about choosing one to use for divination? Most pagan supply shops sell cauldrons. They are often small and specifically intended for magic rather than cookery. They usually look witchy and might be decorated with pentacles. If you want something cheaper – or larger – there are alternatives. The cheapest suggestion is to use an ordinary bowl you already own. I have a few black plastic dishes that once had ready meals in them that I keep for scrying as well as an upcycling effort. These are difficult to recycle because of the pigments used to colour them. Although supermarkets are phasing them out in favour of more environmentally friendly containers, there are still many around. If you have one, don't throw it away. Put it to good use and have a go at scrying in it. Cast-iron cooking pots, casserole dishes or even large mugs are also good. Hunt around your home and see what you already have to improvise with. Charity shops and jumble sales are wonderful places for finding cheap things you can use for witchcraft, including potential scrying bowls. Do check that anything you buy second-hand is watertight if you want to put liquids in it. I managed to soak one scrying class I was teaching because I hadn't realised that I'd filled up a leaky cauldron.

If you want to make like Galadriel and scry outdoors in a silver bowl by moonlight, but you don't have a dresser of sparkly silverware (let's face it, who does?), then charity shops and boot fairs are again your friend. You can often pick up gorgeous vintage silver-plated dishes very cheaply. One of my own fabulous finds is the silver-plated dish supported by three seahorses as legs that you can see in the cover picture. It cost me just a couple of quid, but I feel like a sea priestess when I use it. If you want something large and as much like a traditional cauldron as possible, then look for Potjie pots and Dutch ovens. These are highly versatile cast-iron pots with lids that look like cauldrons and are still used for cooking, particularly outdoors over a campfire. They aren't cheap, but if you want to try scrying into vapour rising above a bubbling cauldron, then cooking pots designed to be used over open flames are essential.

Many witches like to put a silver coin or a crystal in the bottom of their cauldron when scrying into cold water. You can put that in as you fill it, or you can throw the coin or crystal in to watch the ripples it makes to divine meanings. You don't need a special coin; you can use one from your purse that you've cleansed. However, one witch I know has an old silver sixpence, no longer currency, that they keep for this purpose.

Glasses and Goblets

You can also scry into chalices or glasses of water. The nice thing about this is that most people have a wine glass or two in the house, so you don't need to buy anything new. Just fill the glass up with water then use it for scrying. You can place the glass on a dark surface and peer into it, as you would into a cauldron, or you can use the curved sides in the same way you would look into a crystal ball. You can create a dark mirror effect using ink, food colouring, or coffee. If you add colouring agents to clear water, you can look into the swirling patterns for divination too. You can even scry into red wine if you aren't too tempted to drink it before you've finished!

Chapter 6

Scrying with Fire and Smoke

Pyromancy is the ancient art of divination by fire. It's one of the earliest forms of divination, probably practised soon after man first discovered how to set light to things. One can imagine shamans staring into the flames and glowing embers of the fires that warmed our Palaeolithic ancestors, foretelling a good hunt or how well the tribe would fare through winter. In Classical Greece, priestesses at the Temple of Athena in Athens used pyromancy. In Rome, an eternal flame to Vesta, Goddess of Fire and the Hearth, was kept alive by Vestal Virgins. In *Scrying the Secrets of the Future*, Cassandra Eason writes:

> *The Eternal Flame was kept burning until 380 CE. Its priestesses were also fire prophetesses, making offerings to the protective deities of the state... Changes in the pattern of flame and intensity of sacred and festival fires, especially in response to offerings cast on them, indicated the actions of the deities...*

If the fire burned well, the outcome was likely to be good, as well as meaning the offering was well received. In Germany, England and other countries, one Yuletide folk custom going back centuries was to burn a huge log in the fireplace over the entire winter festive period. The way it burnt would be observed and predictions made based on that regarding the year to come. It was considered unlucky if it went out and had to be relit. Real fires were the norm in homes in England until not that long ago, even if fireplaces weren't big enough to keep an entire log burning for 12 nights. Nevertheless, scrying into flames, smoke or embers in the hearth could easily be done in homes on winter nights until about the mid-twentieth century by those who chose to. I used to do it myself in my grandmother's living room when I was young, although she had a coal fire rather than a wood-burning stove. It was one of my favourite ways to scry, and I found it much easier than using that glass fishing float I mentioned earlier. Anthracomancy is a posh term for divining by burning coals, by the way. Staring into a fire, it is easy to get into the appropriate trance-like state and see images in the patterns of light and shadow. In fact, some people find fire scrying much easier than staring into mirrors or crystals, because there is movement within the flames and embers. Kevin Groves writes in 'Scrying': *'I favour mediums where subtle or non-overly rapid change will maintain my attention while still inducing a relaxed meditative state, e.g., cloud, fire, moving water.'*

You can try it around a campfire, fire dish, or bonfire out in the open. In *The Sea Priestess* by Dion Fortune, Morgan Le Fay teaches her apprentice Wilfred to create a Fire of Azrael from driftwood found on the beach. The two of them peer into the embers to see images of the distant past. Morgan adds logs from rare and sacred trees including cedar, sandalwood and juniper to increase the magical effect. Raymond Buckland in his *Complete Book of Witchcraft* also recommends this for scrying by fire to see things of the past, present or future. Nowadays those particular trees are endangered, but if one grows locally to you, you could pick up fallen dead twigs from the ground to add to a fire, while driftwood burns very well on its own. You can add a few drops of essential oils to represent woods for your own Fire of Azrael if you choose, but make sure they are ethically sourced as essential oil production also has an environmental impact. Other trees associated with divination include apple, hazel, oak, rowan and willow.

Preparations and Precautions

Plan carefully before building a fire for scrying. Always check in advance whether open flames are allowed before starting one anywhere. You don't need a huge bonfire just for divination. I would recommend getting something like a fire dish from a garden centre, which is designed to contain any burning material and keep your flames off the ground. Large cast-iron cauldrons can also be used to hold fire as well as to cook things.

Site your fire well away from anything flammable that you don't want to burn. Don't start one under trees, next to garden sheds or fences, at sacred monuments, in high winds or during drought conditions. Never leave your fire unattended. Have heatproof tools, such as tongs, in case you need to tend to bits of burning wood or charcoal, and have a bucket of water, sand or earth ready to put it out. Appoint a responsible adult to keep safety watch, although if you are on your own that will have to be you. Make sure your fire is fully extinguished before leaving and take your fire dish, all your belongings, and any refuse home with you or dispose of it in an appropriate way.

How to Scry into Fire and Smoke

The most basic form of pyromancy involves staring into a fire to watch for patterns and shapes that form in the flames and glowing embers, then interpreting what they mean. A variation on pyromancy is capnomancy, or divination by looking into patterns formed by smoke. As with all forms of scrying, it is good to form a question in your mind first. If you are using essential oils, put them onto the wood before lighting it. Cleanse your space before beginning, ask permission of the spirits of the land, then cast a circle. Start your fire and wait until it is burning well. If you like, you can raise energy by singing, chanting or drumming while the fire is taking hold, but bear in mind that fires need tending too. Herbs can be thrown on after the fire is going. You can choose ones that are appropriate for your question, such as rose petals for a love issue or basil for money matters, or are associated with scrying, such as mugwort or lavender. When it is burning steadily take a few deep breaths to relax, then start to gaze into the flames.

As with other forms of scrying, you might need to spend some watching before anything becomes apparent. Let the warmth of the fire, the crackling of the burning material, and the movement within it help you get into the appropriate state of a light trance. You might get the best results after glowing embers have formed. Look deep within the fire for images, shapes, symbols, and patterns, or alternatively look for flames that attract your interest. Kevin Groves writes: '*I...look into the fire and let my eyes wander until some particular flame shape grabs my attention and then allow the images to unfold.*' Because fire seems alive, you are more likely to see moving and even rapidly changing signs and symbols than with other things. Look out for shapes that recur or which seem to form a sequence.

I always prefer to use intuitive methods of scrying: looking for shapes and symbols that have a personal meaning to me. However, there are traditional meanings associated with the way a fire burns that some use for divination. If it burns brightly and evenly, that is said to be an indication of a good outcome or a positive answer to a question. A fire that struggles to stay alight means it will be more difficult to get what you want or the future will be tough. If a fire that was burning soundly then goes out for no apparent reason, that can indicate an ending. Sparks can indicate bursts of energy and success, important messages that will reach you, or can sometimes mean sparks will fly as in arguments will happen. If the flames burn more in one place than another, or the embers are brighter in one area, that can mean you will need to focus on a specific area in your life more than another. Flickering flames represent uncertainty while twisting flames warn you to beware of unscrupulous people. If a fire burns more strongly than expected then something extraordinary might happen, but be aware that a sudden rise to success can sometimes be followed by a crash. Some people say things to the left generally indicate past influences, the centre is the present and the right is the future. Constantly changing direction or burning erratically can mean upheavals, moves, or a need to change direction. Thin smoke that rises straight upwards is a good sign; smoke that wavers, drifts or billows is an indication of problems.

I should stress that I always urge caution when reading these kinds of traditional meanings into the ways a fire or a candle burn. Usually, these effects are because of something physical such as draughts, dampness, uneven construction, or the quality of material used, rather than supernatural messages. Use your intuition as your primary guide. As always, take notes in your Book of Reflections after you've finished. Thank the spirits of place and say goodbye to any other spirits or deities you have called upon, then open your circle. You might want to have something to eat and drink beside the fire as it burns down to help you ground. Always make sure you have fully extinguished the fire before going and take your litter away with you.

Exercise: Virtual Fire Scrying

If you aren't in position to have a real fire to scry by, try virtual fire scrying. There are a number of videos of real fires burning on YouTube. Pick one that appeals to you and get it running on your phone, tablet or laptop. Put that on your altar, then cleanse and cast a circle around you. Scry into the recorded flames as you would into a real fire. Afterwards, make notes, open your circle, end the recording, and ground properly.

Candle Scrying

Candle flame scrying is the easiest form of pyromancy with a real flame in modern homes without working fireplaces. A candle flame meditation from my earlier book, *Pagan Portals – Candle Magic,* can be used as preparation for psychic work and as a technique for scrying using a flame itself. Always make sure your candle is securely in a holder before you light it. Sit in front of the candle with your eyes open comfortably (not straining to stare too hard). Take three deep breaths. Let the sight of the flame fill your consciousness. It can help to slightly lower your eyelids and defocus your eyes, but do what is comfortable. As you meditate, pay gentle attention to the different parts of the flame.

Candle flames are formed because wax vaporises as it burns. The flame has three zones. The innermost area directly above the wick contains vaporised wax that's not yet burnt. It's the darkest zone. The middle area is yellow and luminous, partly but not entirely burnt, because there's not enough oxygen there to burn away all of the vapour. This is hotter than the innermost zone, but cooler than the outer area. The outer zone is the hottest. The wax vapour is completely combusted. It is a light blue in colour, but not normally visible. Become aware of these three zones – particularly the outer zone, which is the hardest to see. Let your awareness move between these zones and try not to let your attention wander or your thoughts drift off to other things. If they do, gently guide your attention back to the candle flame.

After doing the meditation for a while, see if you can use your psychic senses to scry into those three zones of the candle flame. Spend some time observing the flame through half-closed eyes and see if any shapes or images appear. If you have a specific question, think about that, otherwise try to just empty your mind and watch the flame. You might need to wait some time for anything to happen – at least at first. Do you see shapes? Do they remind you of anything? People or objects perhaps? Even if you don't find images in the flame, you might see some your mind's eye. When you are ready to end the meditation and flame scrying, again take three deep breaths, then extinguish the candle before getting up.

As with scrying into a fire, some people observe the way the flame of a candle burns and give traditional meanings to it in the way I described earlier. Of course, as with bonfires, there can be perfectly rational explanations for candles and flames behaving in certain ways. All candles flicker in a wind, burn more slowly in cold weather and burn faster in hot rooms. A wick that is too small for the size of candle will naturally burn with a slow, low flame, while a wick that is too thick for the width of wax will burn extra fast. Use your common sense as well as any supernatural senses.

Divination by Hot Wax in Water

There is one last thing you can do with tealight candles that you might have used for divination; that is to tip the melted wax into cold water to see what shape forms, then consider what it might symbolise. This type of divination is popular in Scandinavian countries on New Year's Eve, although there it is often done with molten lead using special kits. Carefully pick up your tealight with tongs or tweezers, as you don't want to burn your fingers, then tip the molten wax into a bowl of cold water to see what shape it makes. If you have earlier been scrying with a bowl of water then you can make final use of that too.

Chapter 7

Scrying Outdoors

We touched on outdoor scrying in the last chapter, with fire. Here are other ways to scry outdoors or while looking out into the wider world through our windows. I'm also offering suggestions for daylight divination.

Cloud Scrying

I'm sure everyone at some time has looked up at the clouds in the sky and seen figures, shapes, and patterns in them. You can develop this as a scrying technique to do anywhere you can see clouds, although it's best where there's a big sky, meaning somewhere high up like a cliff or a hilltop, or where the land is flat all around you. Nevertheless, it's perfectly possibly to stare at the clouds from your garden, the local park or out of your window. I once had a very successful scrying session from my bedroom window while ill with flu, although I suspect the feverishness helped. I'm not recommending getting ill as a technique for better scrying...

You don't need to know the types of clouds for general scrying purposes, although if you're weather forecasting that's kind of essential so I'll go into that a bit first. Very simply, little fluffy clouds are known as cumulus. A few small white heaps in a blue sky mean a fine day. Cirrus clouds are thin and wispy. They generally mean fine weather, but possibly changeable. Stratus clouds are blankets covering the sky and can mean drizzle. Grey nimbus clouds are what we think of as rainclouds. However, this book isn't about weather predictions, so I'll get back to discussing how to use clouds for scrying. Cirrus and cumulus clouds are best as it's easiest to spot shapes in them. Make sure you're going to stay warm and dry, so if you are outdoors have something waterproof to lie on and a blanket or coat just in case. Although you can scry at any time of day, personally I find dawn or dusk are best. The low sunlight shining through the clouds casts them into relief and creates more discernible shapes than when the sun is overhead. Never stare directly into the sun as it can damage your eyes.

It's best to lie flat and stare up. Take a few deep breaths and spend some time just tuning in to the general patterns and shapes the clouds are making overhead. Formulate your question in your mind or say it out loud and breathe your words up into the air. Ask the clouds to show you answers to your questions. Then watch and see what unfolds. Take as much time as you can or feel you need. Clouds can change slowly. When you've finished, thank the clouds, make notes, and ground as usual.

Exercise: Cloud Drawing

Grab some pencils and your Book of Reflections. Go outside or look out of a window on a day when there are clouds in the sky. Watch the clouds until you find one that particularly takes your interest. Open your book, get out your pencils, and sketch it. Try to show what interests you about it. You don't have to draw a precise copy of the cloud – in fact you can let your imagination take control. If the cloud looks like something in particular, then emphasise that. Your drawing doesn't have to be a great work of art, but observing the cloud with artist's eyes will help you see the shades and shapes that are useful in scrying.

The Wind in the Trees

My great aunt used to foretell the weather by looking at the way the wind moved the leaves in the trees. Her predictions were often more accurate than anything the weather forecasters said on the radio or TV. I'm not sure if that was her psychic ability or the years she'd spent observing the natural elements while working in her garden. She was a keen gardener with lots of practical knowledge, but all the family thought she had a little green-fingered magic about her too. I asked her to teach me, but I'll be the first to admit I was never as good as her at seeing how a certain twist of a leaf meant a rain shower was on the way, while another movement meant it would blow over. However, I always remember her saying that if the leaves are flipping over completely in the wind, it's time to grab your stuff and go indoors. But that's all weather-forecasting again, so back to real scrying by the trees, to see what's coming.

The first thing, pretty obviously, is to go somewhere there are trees. Ideally this should be a copse or clump. It's best to choose a group of trees you can observe frequently, perhaps in your own garden or through your window. If you regularly work magic in a grove, that's perfect. If there aren't any trees close to you, visit your nearest park or woodland. Choose a day when there's at least some breeze, as the leaves won't be moving much if it's completely calm. Ask permission of the spirits of the trees to watch them and work with them. When you are familiar with the normal movements of the leaves, you can begin to scry. Think of a question and form it in your mind or say it out loud into the wind. Then watch the leaves to observe the patterns they are making. This can also help you get into the right trance-like state of mind. Look for symbols, shapes and pictures in shadows, shades and highlights as the branches move and the leaves shake. I find it helps to half close my eyelids, so the outlines are blurred. Listen too. Cassandra Eason, in *Scrying the Secrets of the Future*, writes:

> Gradually allow your mind to become attuned to the rise and fall of the sound of the wind and the rustling leaves... Before long it will take on the pattern of whispered voices.

Pay attention to everything. Can you smell anything in the air? That can be relevant too. How do you feel about the impressions you are getting? As with all scrying, this is your intuition at work, so pay attention to it. When you've finished, thank the spirits of the trees, then make notes in your Book of Reflections. Afterwards, as always, be sure to ground.

Lakes, Ponds and Pools

I love scrying in rock pools on the beach and by lakes and streams outdoors, but once again I find it easier by moonlight, especially when the moon is full. Rather than kneeling down on the ground to peer into a pool, I take Galadriel's approach, scoop up water in a scrying bowl and use that. Water the moon has touched is considered particularly potent.

Find a suitable spot outdoors next to where clear water flows. Ask permission of the moon and the spirits of place, then cast your circle. Watch for reflections of silvery light and scoop up water from that spot if possible. Sit or stand and scry into its depths. As always, remember to thank the spirits, open your circle and ground afterwards. Return the water to its source. If you don't live anywhere near natural water, then tap water will do. If you visit suitable places you can collect a little spring water and take it home with you, so long as that is permitted. Whenever I visit Glastonbury, I collect water from both the White Spring and the Red Spring for that purpose. You can also make moon water.

Exercise: Making Moon Water

All you need is a clean bottle of clear glass with a secure lid, clean water, and moonlight. Check when there will next be a full moon. Before it rises, fill your bottle with water. Put the lid on and place the bottle where the moonlight will fall on it for as long as possible. This could be outdoors or it could be on a windowsill. Leave the bottle there for the entire night for the moon to charge it with its magical energy. In the morning, put the bottle into the fridge to store for when you want to use your moon water.

Daylight Divination

It's possible to use crystal balls, mirrors and bowls of water to scry in daylight, but it's more difficult in my experience. If I have to scry in bright light, then I've found using an opaque, light-coloured crystal ball works better than a clear one, and a light-coloured water bowl works better than a dark one. To minimise the light, I find it helps to cover my head and the ball or mirror with a dark scarf or shawl. That creates the kind of low-light level that works best for me. There's no doubt that if you get very familiar with using a device, you will find it works for you even in sub-optimum conditions. Also, the more you develop your skills, the better you will be at scrying anywhere and anytime.

Chapter 8

Guided Visualisations

Guided visualisations, sometimes called guided meditations or pathworkings, are great ways of developing intuitive abilities as well as visionary powers. They are journeys we make in our minds using a script or recording that's been created to help us experience a story we're part of. Within those stories what we see is personal to us, and the choices we make are our own. That's how they can help us in all kinds of personal development and magical learning. These visualisations are specifically designed to help develop scrying skills and can be used as ways of scrying in themselves.

Before starting, make sure you're in a safe and comfortable place, where you won't be disturbed. Ideally, guided visualisations are best done with the eyes closed. In a practical sense if you are on your own that means recording each visualisation before you do it for real. You could use your phone or laptop to record it. Play it back to yourself, pausing when necessary in order to fully visualise each part. If that isn't possible, then read each section slowly to yourself, then close your eyes and visualise it as you go.

Within the Crystal Ball

This is a good visualisation to do as a training exercise to improve your scrying ability, or if you don't have a real crystal ball available. However, some people find it easier to scry within a visualisation than with a solid object. That's completely fine – do what works for you.

Close your eyes and relax. Take three deep breaths in and out, in and out, in and out.

Visualise that you are seated at a table on which there is a large crystal ball, a candle and the means to light it, and a wand. The rest of the room you are in is dimly lit and shadowy. Focus on the items on the table. Look at the crystal ball, the candle, and the wand. What do they look like to you? Picture them clearly.

Now, in your mind's eye, light the candle. See its glow illuminate the things on the table, spreading a circle of soft light over the crystal ball and the wand. Look at the flame of your candle. Gently focus your eyes on the flame and feel its light softly falling on you as well. Let the light relax you.

Now, look at the wand. Pick it up. Feel its weight in your hand. With the wand, visualise casting a circle all around yourself, the candle, and the crystal ball. You can trace the outline of the circle of candlelight as it falls on the table, then trace that circle continuing behind you so that you are enveloped in its circumference. It is a circle of protection and you are within its enclosing boundary. You are safe here.

Put the wand down next to the crystal ball. Now move your attention to the ball itself. What does it look like as it stands on the table in the circle of light from the candle?

As you observe the crystal ball, you see a reflection. You see your own face reflected back at you. Observe your reflection. Look into your own eyes as they appear within the crystal ball. Spend some time doing this.

After a while, you begin to realise that your reflection is not exact. There are subtle differences between your reflection and yourself. Observe these differences. What are the differences? What do they mean to you? How do they make you feel? Is there a message for you in them?

Does your reflection want to tell you something? If so, what are they saying? Listen to see if you can hear any words of wisdom or comfort, or suggestions. Is there anything you want to ask?

Perhaps your reflection wants to show you something. Is there anything else to see within the crystal ball? Are there any images, shapes or symbols? If so, look at them, observe them.

Spend some time observing further what is within the crystal ball. After a while, you realise it is time for your scrying to end. Say any final words you wish to say, and listen to any final messages. Thank your reflection for what you have seen and bid them farewell. Then, draw your attention out of the crystal. Look again at the other objects on the table within the circle of candlelight. Pick up the wand again. Trace once more around the circle of protection, but this time visualising the boundary opening up and releasing that which it contained.

Put the wand down and extinguish the candle.

It is now time to return to your normal consciousness. Take three deep breaths in and out. Wiggle your fingers and toes and open your eyes.

Make notes about what you experienced then ground to bring yourself fully back to the everyday world because guided visualisations, like any psychic work, can leave you feeling spacey. You can repeat the visualisation another day if you want.

The Magic Mirror in the Enchanted Tower

This guided visualisation is one I wrote to use in my scrying workshops, but was also included in my earlier book *Pagan Portals: Guided Visualisations*.

Close your eyes and relax. Take three deep breaths in and out, in and out, in and out.

Visualise that you are in a beautiful garden at the edge of a wood. It is a place where you feel safe. Golden afternoon sunlight falls on the flowers in the garden, the weather is pleasantly warm and gentle. Spend time picturing the garden, smelling the scents and listening to any sounds of the birds or the gentle rustling of leaves. If at any time in this meditation you feel unsafe, know that you can return to this safe garden just by wishing it and picturing the garden in your mind's eye – but for now, you are going to leave the safety and sanctity of this delightful garden and venture to find the magic mirror in the enchanted tower.

At the end of the garden is a hedge and in the hedge is a gate that leads into the wood. You know that in the centre of the wood stands an enchanted tower and in the tower is a magic mirror, but only those who are worthy and determined are able to find it. You have decided to try.

Leaving the safety of the garden you go through the gate and enter the wood.

A path winds through the trees and you follow it. Visualise the path and the wood around you. Notice the sights, scents and sounds of the trees, the birds, the animals that live here and be aware of your own movement along the path. What is the path like? Is your going easy or hard? You persevere and continue – unless you decide to turn back of course.

As you progress, the shadows cast by the trees lengthen and you realise it is late afternoon and the sun has started to dip. You keep going along the darkening path. Be aware of the changes to the woodland around you and sky that you glimpse through the canopy of the trees as you go.

It is dusk as the path leads to a clearing, in which there is a tower that reaches higher than the treetops into the purpling sky.

There is a single doorway at the base of the tower. Stop before the door and examine it. What does it look like? How does it open?

You reach out and try opening the door... To your delight – perhaps with ease, or perhaps with difficulty it opens at your touch.

Spiral stairs wind upwards inside the tower and you start to ascend. Around and around you go, higher and higher. Eventually, at the top, the stairs open up in a chamber at the very top of the tower. There are four windows around this chamber, looking out into the night sky in which the stars are clear and a full moon is rising.

The only thing in this room is a full-length mirror on a stand. Move towards the mirror, position yourself in front of it, and look into it. At first all you see is your own reflection and behind you the reflection of the walls of the chamber and a window through which shines the moon.

As you watch, however, the mirror fogs over, then clears again and instead of your reflection you see the someone else. Someone wise and knowing. They are smiling.

'I am the guardian of the mirror,' they say. 'You have found your way here through the woods and found the door to the tower open. You have ascended the tower and made your way here. You are ready to learn the magic of the mirror. What is it that you want to see?'

Decide what you want the mirror to show you. Perhaps it is a place or a person, a scene from the past or from the future, or perhaps it is the answer to a question. Then tell the guardian what it is that you want to see.

Again, the mirror fogs over, and when it clears again you begin to see something else. Allow yourself time for the image or images to form, then watch as you see your vision granted. Continue observing as the vision unfolds.

After some time has passed, the mirror again fogs over, and then clears to show you the wise and knowing guardian of the mirror.

'What you have seen is all that the mirror will show you this night. It is now time for you to leave. You may return again, at other times, to see other visions in the magic mirror, but now you must go.'

And again, the mirror fogs, and clears, and you see your own reflection in the chamber at the top of the tower, but you see the night has ended and the sun is starting to rise through the window behind you. It is dawn.

Leaving the room, you descend the spiral stairs and out through the doorway at the bottom of the tower into the wood. You retrace your way along the path through the wood, back to the gate in the hedge and then into the beautiful and safe garden once more.

When you are ready to return to this normal space and time, take a deep breath, shake yourself a little and open your eyes.

Make notes about what you experienced, then ground to bring yourself fully back to the everyday world.

Chapter 9

Teacup and Coffee Ground Readings

While scrying is often defined as using reflective, refractive or translucent things like mirrors, crystal balls and bowls of water, it can also be done by looking at seemingly random patterns in general; I mentioned fire, clouds and trees earlier, but it can also mean patterns in residues in cups and bowls. Tea-leaf or tea-cup reading was very popular a hundred years ago. In the 1921 book *Tea-Cup Reading*, the Highland Seer wrote: *'It is one of the most common forms of divination practised by the peasants of Scotland and by village fortune-tellers.'* It was also done in London's East End. My father-in-law, a true Cockney, remembers coming home to find his mother reading the leaves at the kitchen table for groups of women eager to learn their fortunes. She poured from the big, brown family teapot into everyday cups: they couldn't afford a fancy set. Problems were aired and gossip was shared as they drank their brew, then she looked at the signs in the dregs to tell them what was to come. I don't know how she learnt the skill, but it was almost certainly a way for a cash-strapped working-class mum to earn a few extra pennies back then.

The Highland Seer felt it was an affordable and homely form of fortune telling: *'Reading the Cup is essentially a domestic form of Fortune-telling to be practised at home, and with success by anyone who will take the trouble to master the simple rules.'* The Seer recommended reading the leaves every morning to see what to expect that day. Plenty of people still like to do a daily reading of some sort, and with many returning to loose tea rather than teabags for environmental reasons, looking into the dregs of a morning drink can be a good alternative to drawing a tarot card. Coffee grounds can be read in a similar way.

Techniques with Tea (and Coffee)

Use loose-leaf tea brewed in a teapot and poured without straining as you obviously need to have leaves to read after you've finished drinking it. Teabags won't work. It's best to use a proper cup of a decent size with a wide opening at the top and smooth, curved sides. I like a vintage china cup, and these can often be picked up cheaply at charity shops and boot fairs if you can't afford a new one. You can use mugs, but the sides are a bit too steep to read the symbols well. It's best if the inside of the cup is plain white as symbols can be obscured by patterns or dark colours. You'll also need a saucer. It doesn't matter if you prefer your tea black or with milk, or with or without sugar. Drink the tea until there's about half a teaspoonful left in the bottom. Then pick it up by the handle and swirl it clockwise, or deosil, three times. Tradition says it should be the left hand. If you have a question, ask it as you do this. If you are drinking real coffee, leave your cup to settle for a while so enough of the grounds remain.

Slowly invert your cup over the saucer and leave it there for a minute or so to let the last of the liquid drain. Then, turn the cup back over again carefully to read the symbols that have formed. Look into the cup and see if you can make out shapes or pictures. Tea leaves tend to clump in small groups that can look like individual symbols. Coffee grounds are much finer and there tends to be a dark brown general background with small symbols among them, or an overall dark pattern.

Traditionally, the position of shapes in the cup is significant. The handle generally represents the querent or person the reading is for. Symbols close to the handle represent things that are very personal, or happening to people who are close or at home. The further away from the handle, the more distant the event portrayed. Timescale can be represented by how far down the cup the symbol appears. Things near the rim are immediate while things at the bottom are further into the future. However, in my experience I've found the position doesn't always represent time and space, especially when I'm not trying to foretell the future. If I want insight into a personal issue, symbols near the top can represent more superficial aspects of the issue, while things further down are more deeply significant or hidden. You can also read shapes in the saucer if it isn't overflowing with liquid. Some say the saucer best represents matters of the heart. As with any form of scrying, make notes of what you see. With cup reading you can photograph the shapes formed to refer to later. Grounding is less of an issue with teacup or coffee-ground readings, but by all means have a biscuit to go with your drink if you fancy it.

Making out Patterns

Unlike with crystal balls, you will definitely either see some leaves or no leaves in your cup. There might be just a few, or there might be a large number, but the shapes they form can look like a meaningless mass or vague sprinkling at first. View the cup from all sides and angles. It can take time to make out anything recognisable. Even the Highland Seer writes: *'It is not very easy at first to see what the shapes really are, but after looking at them carefully they become plainer.'* Some books on tea-leaf reading give pictorial examples, but I find they can be confusing as the shapes in your cup will probably look nothing like the book's images. What they mean to you is important, not how close they are to some artist's representation of, say, buildings or animals or people.

You might see lines, circles, squares or crosses, or shapes that are recognisable. You might see letters or numbers. Make a note of their size as well as their position as the larger they are, the more substantial or important their significance. Sometimes there will be just one large picture in the cup; sometimes lots of little symbols. Things close together might have a connected meaning. They could be two specific beings or objects that are related, like a witch and their cat, or they might symbolise a condition, like a cloud over someone's head meaning they are unhappy. Lines between things or arrows pointing towards things can represent travel and directions, or arrivals and meetings. These images are stationary and need symbols to show movement, whereas things you see in crystal balls or fires can be moving.

As with any form of scrying, what a pattern or symbols means to you is far more relevant than any traditional interpretation you can look up. However, our culture and background – and correspondences given to symbols in any magical traditions we follow – can very much influence what things mean to us. With tea-cup reading, the way the leaves naturally group means certain types of shapes are more likely to occur than others and have been ascribed particular interpretations in the past. As with tarot, you can follow tradition, or you can use your intuition. The next chapter is all about interpretation of shapes and symbols.

Exercise: Develop a Morning Ritual

Find a cup and saucer you are going to use every morning for practising tea or coffee reading, as well as loose-leaf tea or ground coffee and a teapot or cafetiere. Cleanse your cup thoroughly. On the first morning, get up at around dawn (this is of course easier in the winter months). Brew your tea or coffee in a mindful fashion, paying attention while you make it, savouring the experience. Hold your empty cup up so the rays of the early morning sun flow over it and into it. Keep your eyes on the cup and watch the light on it (don't stare at the sun). Ask the sun to bless your cup and grant that it shows you true readings. Continuing to be mindful and paying full attention to what you are doing, pour your tea or coffee into the cup. Sip your drink, savouring it. Ask what the day ahead will bring. When very little brew is left, take the cup in your left hand and turn it clockwise three times. Slowly invert your cup over the saucer and let the liquid drain. Turn the cup right side up and do your reading.

Make notes and sketch pictures of what you see in your Book of Reflections. Do this every morning as a ritual for a week.

Chapter 10

Interpreting Shapes and Symbols

Sometimes what you see in your crystal ball or coffee cup is just what it looks like. Perhaps you recognise a real person, place or situation and can identify what's going on and know what it means. However, sometimes it might seem symbolic rather than realistic. You need to interpret the shapes and signs. Cultural backgrounds and our own personal experiences make a difference. The same symbol can also mean different things to a person at different times in their lives or in answer to different questions. Although it's tempting to want a book that gives all the answers, we usually have to use our own intuition when interpreting what we scry. The feelings we get are as important as the symbol itself. What mood or emotion does the symbol stir? Is it reassuring or is it an alert?

The context is important too. If you asked a specific question, that will be relevant, but other things happening in your life could affect what you see. For example, a bell might symbolise a wedding or other celebration, but it could also be an alarm, a phone call or a doorbell. If you run a shop, a tinkling bell might indicate customers. When I was a child, a bell was rung to signal the end of playtime and the start of lessons. Bells ring out on holy days or at sacred times in many religions. Meanings can change too. For the Highland Seer a hundred years ago, a kettle meant risk of death, but I doubt many people would identify with that in the twenty-first century. For Jane Struthers in *The Art of Tea-Leaf Reading*, published in 2006, a kettle means a happy home.

Nevertheless, it can help to consider ways symbols have been interpreted by others as well as what they mean to us. The list that follows offers some possible meanings for common symbols, but these are just a starting point for interpretations. Always ask yourself if the description feels right for you. If it doesn't, think further. If your question is about a health or finance matter you should consult a qualified professional such as a doctor or financial advisor. No form of divination or fortune telling should ever be taken as advice. It's purely something to think about. The future is not fixed. As in the words of Galadriel, the magic mirror shows things that may be, not things that will definitely come to pass.

A List of Symbols

For the meanings in the following list, I considered different interpretations from various sources and traditions as well as my own personal experience. Use this as a start if you feel you need help in finding your own interpretations of what you see, but no list is ever completely exhaustive.

Acorn: The start of a project or an idea; saving money; an investment; good health; fecundity; protection; good fortune in general.

Aircraft: Travel; a person from abroad; a holiday; reaching for the sky; projects with both good and bad aspects.

Anchor: Stability and security; feeling stuck; staying grounded; a safe place; a boat journey; good luck.

Angel: Good news; spiritual protection.

Animal: In general, trust your instincts, but try to work out what animal it is.

Apples: Health; long life; temptation; love and sex; worldly experience; bountiful harvests. Mythological meanings include the Garden of Eden, the judgement of Paris and the Isle of Avalon. They are associated with Aphrodite, Eris, and Eve.

Arch: An opening; a journey; support or shelter.

Arrow: Hitting a target; movement (up, down, sideways, onwards or backwards); disagreeable communication; defence; pain (emotional or physical); a direction; fatherhood; Sagittarius in astrology.

Axe: Overcoming difficulties; tools or weapons; destruction; transformation; creation. The labrys, or double axe, is the symbol of Minoan Goddesses, representing the butterfly of change and rebirth.

Baby: Birth; a new start; a creative project; listen to your inner child.

Badger: Prosperity; family life; the night; self-defence. Traditionally badgers represented bachelors in tea-cup readings.

Basket: Shopping; a gift; fruitfulness.

Bat: The night; darkness; keen hearing; manoeuvring by instinct; mystery; facing fears. In folklore, bats are associated with vampires. They represent the soul in some cultures.

Bear: Strength; cunning; ferocity; protective motherhood. In mythology they can symbolise resurrection and rebirth. Bears are associated with the Goddesses Artemis/Diana and Artio.

Bees: Productivity; teamwork; avoid being stung; messages from the spirit world.

Bell: A wedding or other celebration; a warning; a phone call; a call to work, lessons, or prayers; energetic cleansing and protection.

Birds: In general, a lucky sign; travel, perhaps abroad or by air. Also consider the type of bird.

Boat: Travel by water; moving on; dealing with emotional issues.

Books: Knowledge; learning; writing. Can you identify the title, subject or content of the book, or is it a blank notebook?

Bouquet: Luck; friendship; success; marriage; celebration.

Bridge: A journey; making up after a quarrel; change or transition. In mythology a bridge represents communicating with the spirit world.

Broom: A fresh start; physical and spiritual cleansing.

Bull: Male strength; virility; power; also, brute force; anger; destructiveness; a difficult situation. In Minoan mythology the sacred bull was associated with their God, who the Greeks turned into the monstrous Minotaur in the labyrinth. It can mean facing fears, and initiation. Taurus in astrology.

Butterfly: Success; pleasure; flirting; impulsiveness; inability to settle; transformation; the soul.

Candle: Illumination; mystery; spiritual observances; avoid getting burnout; unrequited love.

Car: A journey, a visit, being in control or being taken for a ride.

Castle: Security; history; a legacy.

Cat: Independence; treachery; psychic powers; witchcraft; good luck; pleasure. In mythology, cats are associated with the Goddess Bastet.

Centaur: Healing; knowledge; Sagittarius in astrology (also see arrow).

Chain: Addiction; restrictions; struggles for freedom; troubles.

Chair: A new colleague or new job; a visitor; support; time to rest.

Church: Christian traditions; life rites.

Circle: Money; the sun; a ring; the end of a cycle; the circle of life; eternity; unity; protection.

Clock: Time; an appointment; delays.

Clouds: Trouble; lack of clarity; caution; seek professional advice.

Clover: Good luck.

Comet: Great success; rapid change; trouble.

Compass: Travel; indication of directions east, south, west or north.

Cow: Motherhood; plenty. Cows are sacred in many religions and can represent mother Goddesses.

Crab: Emotional insecurity; defensiveness. Cancer in astrology.

Cross: A warning; delay; no entry. In mythology a cross is both a solar symbol and a Christian symbol.

Crown: Success; honour; promotion.

Crystals: Clarity, psychic power; treasure; jewels; the element of earth. The type of crystals will indicate further meanings.

Dagger: Betrayal; trouble; conflict; two-edged situations. As an athame, used in witchcraft and magic to cast a protective circle. As a knife, can be a tool as well as a weapon.

Deer: Endurance; longevity; disputes; the hunter and the hunted. Does are associated with meekness. In mythology, stags are associated with Cernunnos and Herne.

Dice: Chance; games; avoid risks.

Dog: Faithful friends; guardians; adversaries. The breed of dog can be relevant.

Dove: Peace; reconciliation; purity, spirit; good luck.

Dragon: Big changes; difficulties with great reward; forces of nature; the elements; wisdom; strength; power; greed; destruction; powerful adversaries; spiritual guardians; initiation; facing fears.

Duck: Superficiality; fidelity; keeping afloat.

Eagle: Honour; status; wealth; protection; destruction. Represents spirituality in many religions.

Eggs: Fertility; start of something new.

Elephant: Good luck; good health; longevity; long memory; environmental issues.

Eyes: Be vigilant; protection; someone watching you; be truthful with yourself.

Faces: Someone you know or will meet. Consider who the person is. Pay attention to the expression.

Feather: Spiritual truth; messages from spirit; the element of air. Pay attention to the colour or whether you can identify the bird it came from.

Fish: Intuition; emotional issues; emigration. If you can tell the type of fish, carp indicates longevity; salmon mean wisdom. Pisces in astrology.

Flag: A warning; taking sides; a cause.

Flowers: In general: happiness; success; marriage; nature (also see bouquet). The type of flower will affect the meaning.

Fox: Trickery; craftiness; cunning.

Frog: Success; transformation; fertility; an unlikely romance. The Goddess Heket.

Gate: Blockages; obstacles, openings; transitions; protection; a portal.

Goat: Virility; lewdness; creativity; misfortune; hardiness. Capricorn in astrology.

Gun: Discord; conflict; anger; danger.

Hammer: Triumph over adversity; perseverance. The God Thor.

Hand: Friendship; fate; help; protection; crafting or manual work. Gestures will affect the meaning.

Hare: A journey; the return of an absent friend; sexuality; hope; cycles of nature; witchcraft. Lunar deities.

Harp: The ancestors; music; love.

Hat: Success; promotion. The type can indicate a specific role or person in that role.

Heart: Love; emotions; relationships.

Horse: Strength; teamwork; endurance; a journey. The Goddesses Rhiannon and Epona.

Horseshoe: Good luck; success; protection; marriage.

Hourglass: Time; urgency; a warning.

House: Security; success; home life; moving home.

Humans: People important to you; people who will enter your life; visitors. Also judge them by what they are doing or wearing.

Ivy: Faithful friends; Yuletide. The God Dionysus.

Jug: Sharing hospitality; good health. In astrology, a jug bearer is the sign for Aquarius.

Kettle: A happy home; comfort in sad times; things coming to a boil.

Key: Doors opening; a new home; romance; finding a solution.

Kite: Travel; flying high; being in control; the element of air.

Knife: Quarrels; surgical procedures; having the tools to cut through problems, the witch's athame (also see dagger).

Ladder: Promotion; career move; self-improvement; hopes; climbing; fear of falling.

Letters: Envelopes traditionally mean news; a need to communicate. Letters of the alphabet often relate to the other things seen, or people's initials.

Lightning: Sudden realisation; inspiration; a warning; storms.

Lines: Connections; journeys; long life. Straight lines mean things might be direct or straightforward; wavy lines can mean difficulties. If the lines form a shape or pattern, that will be important.

Lion: Bravery; strength; fierceness; help from a powerful friend. Leo in astrology.

Mermaid: Trickery; emotional entanglement.

Money: Check your finances; savings; money is on the way.

Monkey: Trickery; secret enemies; problem solving; perseverance.

Moon: Mystery; illusion; women's issues; fortune; magic and witchcraft. The phase of the moon can also indicate when something will happen or whether something is increasing in strength, at full power, or waning. Lunar Goddesses include Selene/Luna and Artemis/Diana.

Mountain: A challenge; powerful friends; powerful enemies; a spiritual journey.

Mouse: Poverty; uninvited visitors; quietly overcoming obstacles.

Mushroom: A quarrel; increased prosperity; connection with nature.

Nest: A new home; settling down; saving money.

Numbers: Read these in connection with your question or what you see with them.

Oak: Strength; endurance; long life; good health; good luck; a gateway to other realms.

Owl: Wisdom; the night; mystery; witchcraft; bringers of messages; guardian of the underworld; caution; traditionally bad luck. The Goddesses Blodeuwedd and Athena.

Palm tree: A journey abroad; a holiday.

Parrot/parakeet: Communication; noisy chatter; colourful company; travel.

Peacock: Success; love; marriage; vanity. The Goddess Hera.

Pen: Writing; check official documents carefully before signing them.

Pentagram: For witches, this represents the four elements and spirit. The Goddess Venus, and the five wounds of Christ, in mythology. A pentacle is a pentagram in a circle, representing eternity and protection.

Pig: Good and bad luck mixed; a faithful lover; envious friends; fertility; greed. The Great Mother Goddess.

Pigeons: Traditionally news if flying; domestic bliss if resting.

Pine tree: Happiness; Yuletide; immortality. The God Dionysus and the Goddess Cybele.

Question mark: Uncertainty; ask more questions; worries; surprises.

Rabbit: Good luck; fertility; innocence; the moon.

Rainbow: Wishes; diversity; hope; an end to troubles; messages from the Gods.

Ram: Sexuality; wild behaviour (although sheep are traditionally seen as the opposite). The God Pan. Aries in astrology.

Rat: Rat has mixed meanings from culture to culture, including betrayal; pestilence; prudence; industriousness; prosperity.

Raven: Warning of danger. The God Bran.

Ring: Marriage; engagement (see also circle).

Rose: Love; romance; happiness; secrecy; socialism. The Goddesses Aphrodite and Venus.

Scales: Justice; a lawsuit; balance. Libra in astrology.

Scissors: Quarrels; cutting connections with people.

Scorpion: Treachery; stings; endings; guardians.

Scorpio in astrology.

Shark: Danger; beware of predatory people.

Sheep: Success; prosperity; shyness; lack of independent thought (rams are traditionally the opposite).

Shells: A holiday; the seaside; romance. The Goddess Venus.

Snakes: Caution; spiteful enemies; difficulties; health issues; sexuality; rebirth. In mythology, the snake Ouroboros represents eternity.

Spider: Money coming in; connectedness; entanglement; fate; feminine power.

Spirals: History repeating itself; the ancestors; cycles of life, death and rebirth; gaining self-knowledge.

Squares: If solid, a blockage; if open; possibilities.

Star: Good luck; fame; success; fortune; happiness; destiny.

Sun: Success; summer; daytime; joy; light; energy; be more positive. The God Apollo.

Swan: Good luck; fidelity; protection; serenity in the face of hard work; transformation.

Sword: Disputes; quarrels; victory. A broken sword can mean defeat.

Telephone: A message; communication; a reminder to get in touch with someone.

Toad: Deceit; unexpected enemies; unexpected allies. Toads are also associated with traditional witchcraft.

Train: Travel; progress; being on the right track. A missed or delayed train is the opposite.

Trees: Good luck; spend more time in nature; ancestors. The type of tree will affect the reading. In mythology, the world tree connects the Earth with the spiritual and ancestral realms.

Triangle: Good luck; relationship issues.

Twins: Soul mates; siblings; look at both sides of an issue. Gemini in astrology.

Umbrella: Trouble; shelter; savings.

Unicorn: Purity; innocence.

Vulture: Bitter rivals; difficult times.

Wheat: Prosperity; abundance; harvest time. In astrology, the sign for Virgo is a young woman holding a sheaf of wheat.

Wheel: An inheritance; a time of change; fortune; the Wheel of the Year.

Wine glass or bottle: A party or celebration; temperance.

Wings: Protection; a message from afar or from spirit; success in a venture. In mythology, wings symbolise the angels.

Wolf: Intrigue; hardship; cunning; a call to get in touch with your wilder nature. The God Mars.

Yew tree: Old age; burial grounds; the ancestors.

Zebra: Adventures; holidays.

A List of Colours

Not everyone sees colours when they scry, and if you are using tea leaves you will probably only see the colours of the leaves or cup. However, colours can have significance. As before, the way it feels when you see it and your own associations are more important than traditional interpretations, but you can use the following list as a start.

Red: Passion; sex; love courage; fire; basic material needs.

Pink: Romantic love; friendship; emotional wellbeing.

Orange: Energy; encouragement; physical desires; recovery after a set-back or break-up.

Yellow: Cheerfulness; creativity; communication; happiness; the sun; wealth; fruitful harvest; power; control.

Brown: Earth; animals.

Green: Nature; environmental issues; the Earth; health; wealth; love; luck.

Blue: Communication; spirituality; peace; harmony; dreams; sea and sky.

Indigo: Intuition; psychic abilities.

Purple: Social status; legal matters.

Violet: Wisdom; spirituality.

Grey: Neutrality; balance; mists.

Black: Purification; protection; hidden things; mourning and honouring the dead.

White: Purity; peace; protection; the moon.

Gold: Prosperity and solar influences.

Silver: Prosperity and lunar influences.

Times and Dates

Various symbols can indicate when things might happen. I tend to see astrological signs relating to times of the year, but not everyone will find that useful. Keen gardeners or herbalists might see the flowers that are in bloom in that season, others might see the first letter of the appropriate month. You might see numbers to represent times of day, or you might even see the hands of a clock. When you are asking questions relating to times and dates it is particularly important to note it in your Book of Reflections so you can check later to see if what you predicted came to pass.

Chapter 11

Problem Solving and Frequently Asked Questions

Here are some frequently asked questions with answers that might help if you are experiencing problems with scrying.

It Just Isn't Working for Me, What Should I Do?

It can take lots of time and practise to find a method that works. If you've turned to this section before reading the rest of the book, then go back and do that. Try out every method and do all the exercises. You don't have to master every kind of scrying; if one or two methods work for you while others don't, practise the things you find more effective. Maybe you can see things within a ball or mirror in a guided visualisation, but not in a physical ball or mirror. That's also completely okay. You can always go back and try other things again later.

Don't give up if the first or second attempt don't work. I would recommend setting a regular routine. You could scry for ten minutes every day for a month, perhaps starting on the eve of the full moon and continuing until just after the next full moon. Some nights of the year are traditional times for scrying, including the evening before May Day or Beltane, Midsummer's Eve, Halloween or Samhain, the evening before the Winter Solstice and New Year's Eve. You could make a resolution to scry at one of those special times and use the power of tradition to help your efforts. Another thing is to vary the time of day you look into your crystal ball or mirror, as that can make a big difference to some people. The phase of the moon can be important. Many witches find it easiest to scry at the full moon, while others prefer the new moon. Practise and experimentation will help you discover your own best ways of scrying.

I've Seen Something Scary, What Does it Mean?

Sometimes we might see things that look scary when we scry. It's quite okay to not want to. If you cast a circle to keep out unwanted influences, they won't harm you. As I mentioned earlier, if you see something you don't want to contemplate while you are scrying, one technique is to say: *'Leave this crystal (or cauldron or whatever), go in peace, be gone.'* This can often move the thing on. If it doesn't, you can end the scrying session earlier than you otherwise intended and try again another time or with another method. One thing I would emphasise is that if you are experiencing emotional issues, avoid scrying until you feel better. If it continues or is worrying you, or you have psychological problems, seek professional help from your GP or counsellor.

There are other things you can do to minimise the chances of seeing something scary. The phase of the moon can affect it. Some people say you shouldn't scry or do any magical work at the dark moon for that reason. Personally, I've found the dark moon can be a good time to look into the dark to search for things that are hidden, but sometimes hidden things are also things that can upset us. If you want to avoid that, try a different moon phase.

If you do see something troubling, I want to reassure you that it rarely means doom and gloom. Sometimes the crystal ball or mirror reflects our fears so we can understand them better. This is part of shadow work and is something many witches feel is an important part of personal development. Back in chapter 4 I described a scrying session in which I saw an owl and then a dragon flying towards me. Owls can symbolise bad luck and dragons can symbolise destruction. After initially feeling scared, I realised this was a message for me to face my fears and overcome them. Dragons can be powerful spiritual allies as well as fire-breathing monsters. In fact, many of the things we are most fearful of can also be things that will help us in our personal development. And our fears don't always come to pass.

Let me tell you a story. When my grandmother was young, she worked with the famous astrologer, Alan Leo, who was also psychic. He told her he was worried about what would happen to her at the end of her life. He said he saw her *'standing alone amidst desolation'*. All her life she was scared of this vision of her future. It came true, but it wasn't that bad at all. In the 1960s and 1970s my local council decided to demolish large areas of old houses and replace them with new estates and an industrial park. They called it 'slum clearance' and started compulsory purchasing people's homes, including where I lived with my mum, dad, grandma and grandad. We didn't want to move. Our house might have been run down and without mod cons, but it wasn't a slum to us. We found a solicitor to fight our case, and we held out until our house was the last one standing in the entire street. All the others had been demolished. The council, desperate to knock our house down, offered my family a higher price than our 'slum' was worth to get us to agree to go. We accepted.

One morning, when we were packing our last boxes of possessions and getting ready to move to our new home, my mum looked out of grandma's bedroom window and pointed to some graffiti scrawled on a hoarding over the road. It read: *'Desolation row.'* So, the prediction came true, as our house was indeed standing alone amidst desolation, but it wasn't the awful thing my grandma had feared all those years as we were looking forward to a fresh start. As I explain in the next section, I don't believe the future is completely fixed, but this story demonstrates that even if you truly see the future, it won't necessarily happen in quite the way you think it will.

Is the Future Fixed?

This question has been endlessly debated for millennia, but as I've stated, I don't believe the future is fixed. What you see is perhaps a possible outcome, but it can also be a warning about what might happen if you don't take sensible precautions. I've heard quite a few stories of people seeing accidents happen when doing divination, but choosing to take a different path and being completely unharmed. Forewarned is fore-armed, as the saying goes. As the example I mentioned earlier shows, even if a prediction does turn out to be true, it might not have the impact you think it will. However, my experience is that futures seen in crystal are definitely not set in stone. Sometimes, as I explained just now, we are seeing our fears rather than anything real. We can also see things we want or hope for, giving us insights into our own minds rather than what is to come.

What Should I Do About Lingering Energies?

Sometimes people are concerned that using scrying devices might attract unwanted energies, and that perhaps they might linger afterwards. Obviously, no one wants house guests of any kind that have outstayed their welcome. You shouldn't have problems if you follow the cleansing and protection instructions I described before scrying, and dismiss any entities when you finish. However, if you do feel something nasty or unpleasant of a spiritual nature is hanging around your home, then going through the cleansing procedures again should clear that up. Have a bath in which salt has been added. Really soak in the bath and make sure you wash yourself all over, including rinsing your hair. Then clean your entire home both physically by dusting and running the vacuum cleaner around, as well as using any of the energy cleansing methods I described: sweeping with a besom, smoke cleansing, sprinkling salty water, or cleansing with light. You can also ring a bell in each room of your home. Open your front door and tell the unwanted visitor it is time for them to leave. You should cleanse any crystal balls, mirrors or other devices again thoroughly as well. David Salisbury, in his book *A Mystic Guide to Cleansing and Clearing,* explains that you can use scrying techniques to help with cleansing. He writes:

I like to scry when I'm working on clearing entities out of a space. I will usually gaze into my black mirror and ask that the image of the entity appear before me. If the type of entity is unknown, sometimes scrying for it will help me figure it out.

Knowing what the unwanted visitor is, makes it easier to ask it to leave. Visualise it going out of your front door and back to wherever it came from. Those things should do the trick. If you still feel your house needs further cleansing, then repeat the processes, either at the time of the full moon when magic is at its most effective, or when it just begins to wane, which is a time for banishing.

Where are the Messages Coming From?

Some practitioners say visions that come when scrying are from our subconscious or our imagination, others say they come from deities, spirits, angels, other supernatural external agents, some believe we are psychically tuning in to the universe. My own personal view is that it can be a mixture of all those things. You don't need to be psychic to scry, although it can certainly help. You don't need to contact spirits – unless you choose to. I believe scrying can be thought of as a tool for self-knowledge, giving us messages from our own subconscious minds. It can help us consider the best course forward in life, overcome indecision, and understand what will make us happiest by knowing ourselves better.

What Should I do to Scry for Others?

This book has been about scrying for yourself, but you can ask questions on behalf of others if they ask you. It helps to have them present with you. Get them to ask their question, then repeat it yourself as you gaze into the crystal ball, mirror, tea leaves or whatever. If you are scrying for others, think about the ethics of what to tell them. Don't go about prophesying doom or offering medical or financial advice if you aren't qualified to do so. It's also worth bearing in mind that in the past, according to Professor Ronald Hutton, many cunning folk would actually get their clients to look into the crystal ball, mirror or bowl of water to see their own answers to their questions. The wise man or wise woman wouldn't do the scrying themselves – they would put the client into a light trance and guide them to help themselves. That's a technique that can still be used today.

Last Words

When the hobbits return to the Shire at the end of *The Lord of the Rings,* they discover that what was seen in the Mirror of Galadriel has come to pass. Destructive forces are at work there. However, what they had learnt and experienced on their journey had more than ably equipped them to deal with those problems. They had faced their fears and gained insights into their hidden strengths, and quickly deal with troublemakers in their homeland. Those are also aspects of personal development that can be gained through regularly practising scrying. We are all on our own journeys through life and we all sometimes face struggles that seem hard, but we can find within ourselves the strengths we need to go on and overcome them. Knowledge – particularly self-knowledge – is part of that.

Yes, *The Lord of the Rings* is a work of fiction set in a fantastical land full of magic and mythical creatures; sometimes the visions we see when scrying might also seem fantastical. Fantastical things are full of symbolism that can resonate with us on a deeper level than things of the mundane world. That is one of the mysteries of magic that scrying can reveal. I hope your explorations into the worlds revealed in your crystal ball or mirror, in the depths of water or flame, in clouds or in the grounds of your coffee, show you all the wonders you wish were revealed, and help you in whatever adventures your future holds.

Bibliography

'A Highland Seer', *Tea-Cup Reading, and the Art of Fortune-Telling by Tea Leaves*, viewed at Project Gutenberg

Anderson, Stephen Warde, *The Anderson Revisionist Bible: The Books of Moses*, Lulu

Brown, Colette, *How to Read an Egg: Divination for the Easily Bored*, O-Books

Buckland, Raymond, *Complete Book of Witchcraft*, Llewellyn

Butler, W.E, *How to Develop Clairvoyance*, The Aquarian Press

Caroll, Lewis, *Through the Looking Glass: And What Alice Found There*, viewed at Google Books

Cerqueira, Fábio Vergara, 'Erotic Mirrors. Eroticism in the Mirror. An Iconography of Love in Ancient Greece (fifth to fourth century B.C.)' at www.researchgate.net

Cunningham, Scott, *Cunningham's Encyclopedia of Magical Herbs*, Llewellyn

Davies, Owen, 'Divination', in *Harry Potter: A History of Magic*, British Library/Bloomsbury

Davis, Owen (ed), *The Oxford Illustrated History of Witchcraft and Magic*, Oxford University Press

Draco, Melusine, *Pagan Portals – Divination: By Rod, Birds and Fingers*, Moon Books

Eason, Cassandra, *Scrying the Secrets of the Future: How to Use Crystal Ball, Fire, Wax, Mirrors, Shadows, and Spirit Guides to Reveal Your Destiny*, New Page Books

Eason, Cassandra, 'Mirror Scrying: Hathor Mirror Magic', viewed at www.cassandraeason.com/divination/mirror_magic.htm

Fortune, Dion, *The Sea Priestess*, Weiser Books

Gauding, Madonna, *The Signs and Symbols Bible*, Godsfield

Garner, Alan, *The Owl Service*, HarperCollins

Groves, Kevin, 'Scrying', viewed at temple.houseofkiya.co.uk/wp-content/uploads/2014/08/ArtemisGathering2014.pdf

Hall, Judy, *The Crystal Bible*, Godsfield

Hannant, Sara, *Of Shadows: One Hundred Objects from the Museum of Witchcraft and Magic*, Strange Attractor Press

Le Breton, Mrs John, *The White Magic Book*, Pearson

O'Neill, Barbara, 'Reflections of Eternity: An Overview on Egyptian Mirrors from Prehistory to the New Kingdom', viewed at http://www.Egyptological.com

Page, Sophie; 'Love in a Time of Demons' in *Spellbound: Magic, Ritual and Witchcraft*, Ashmolean

Parker, Julia and Derek, *The Secret World of Your Dreams*, Piatkus

Roud, Steve, *The Penguin Guide to the Superstitions of Britain and Ireland*, Penguin

Salisbury, David, *A Mystic Guide to Cleansing and Clearing*, Moon Books

Shakespeare, *Macbeth*, viewed at Project Gutenberg

Starza, Lucya, *Pagan Portals – Guided Visualisations*, Moon Books

Starza, Lucya, *Pagan Portals – Candle Magic*, Moon Books

Struthers, Jane, *The Art of Tea-Leaf Reading*, Godsfield

Tolkien, JRR, *The Lord of the Rings*, HarperCollins

Valiente, Doreen, *An ABC of Witchcraft: Past and Present*, Phoenix

Pagan Portals - Candle Magic
A witch's guide to spells and rituals

978-1-78535-043-6 (Paperback)
978-1-78535-044-3 (e-book)

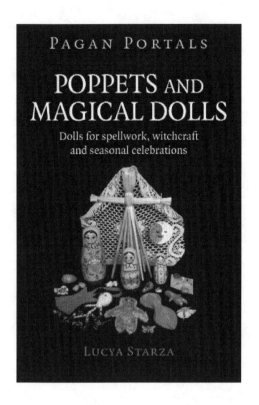

Pagan Portals - Poppets and Magical Dolls

Dolls for spellwork, witchcraft and seasonal celebrations

978-1-78535-721-3 (Paperback)
978-1-78535-722-0 (e-book)

Pagan Portals - Guided Visualisations
Pathways into Wisdom and Witchcraft

978-1-78904-567-3 (Paperback)
978-1-78904-568-0 (e-book)

**MOON
BOOKS**

PAGANISM & SHAMANISM

What is Paganism? A religion, a spirituality, an alternative
belief system, nature worship? You can find support for all these
definitions (and many more) in dictionaries, encyclopaedias, and
text books of religion, but subscribe to any one and the truth will
evade you. Above all Paganism is a creative pursuit, an encounter
with reality, an exploration of meaning and an expression of the
soul. Druids, Heathens, Wiccans and others, all contribute their
insights and literary riches to the Pagan tradition. Moon Books
invites you to begin or to deepen your own encounter, right here,
right now.
If you have enjoyed this book, why not tell other readers by
posting a review on your preferred book site.

Medicine for the Soul
The Complete Book of Shamanic Healing
Ross Heaven
All you will ever need to know about shamanic healing and how to
become your own shaman...
Paperback: 978-1-78099-419-2 ebook: 978-1-78099-420-8

Shaman Pathways – The Druid Shaman
Exploring the Celtic Otherworld
Danu Forest
A practical guide to Celtic shamanism with exercises and
techniques as well as traditional lore for exploring the Celtic
Otherworld.
Paperback: 978-1-78099-615-8 ebook: 978-1-78099-616-5

Traditional Witchcraft for the Woods and Forests
A Witch's Guide to the Woodland with Guided Meditations and
Pathworking
Mélusine Draco
A Witch's guide to walking alone in the woods, with guided
meditations and pathworking.
Paperback: 978-1-84694-803-9 ebook: 978-1-84694-804-6

Wild Earth, Wild Soul
A Manual for an Ecstatic Culture
Bill Pfeiffer
Imagine a nature-based culture so alive and so connected,
spreading like wildfire. This book is the first flame...
Paperback: 978-1-78099-187-0 ebook: 978-1-78099-188-7

Naming the Goddess
Trevor Greenfield
Naming the Goddess is written by over eighty adherents and
scholars of Goddess and Goddess Spirituality.
Paperback: 978-1-78279-476-9 ebook: 978-1-78279-475-2

Shapeshifting into Higher Consciousness
Heal and Transform Yourself and Our World with Ancient
Shamanic and Modern Methods
Llyn Roberts
Ancient and modern methods that you can use every day to
transform yourself and make a positive difference in the world.
Paperback: 978-1-84694-843-5 ebook: 978-1-84694-844-2

Readers of ebooks can buy or view any of these bestsellers by
clicking on the live link in the title. Most titles are published in
paperback and as an ebook. Paperbacks are available in traditional
bookshops. Both print and ebook formats are available online.

Find more titles and sign up to our readers' newsletter at
http://www.johnhuntpublishing.com/paganism
Follow us on Facebook at https://www.facebook.com/MoonBooks
and Twitter at https://twitter.com/MoonBooksJHP